D1301421

What's Next, Gen X?

What's Next, Gen X?

KEEPING UP,
MOVING AHEAD,
and GETTING
the CAREER YOU WANT

Tamara Erickson

HARVARD BUSINESS PRESS
Boston, Massachusetts

Printed in the United States of America

14 13 12 11 10 5 4 3 2 1

Library of Congress Cataloging-in-Publication Data

Erickson, Tamara J., 1954-
What's next, Gen X? : keeping up, moving ahead, and getting the career you want / Tamara Erickson.
p. cm.
ISBN 978-1-4221-2064-4 (hbk. : alk. paper) 1. Generation X—Employment.
2. Career development. I. Title.
HF5381.E5855 2010
650.14—dc22

2009005483

The paper used in this publication meets the requirements of the American National Standard for Permanence of Paper for Publications and Documents in Libraries and Archives Z39.48-1992.

To Kate Burnham

XoX

TABLE OF CONTENTS

Acknowledgments *ix*

Introduction *xi*

Part I You as a Generation

Chapter 1 Shaping Generation X: Your Teen Years 3

Chapter 2 Taking Stock: Generation X Today 21

Chapter 3 *What* Are They Thinking?: The Other Four Generations 43

Part II Evaluate Your Next Steps

Chapter 4 What Do *You* Want?: Resetting Your Life and Work Priorities 63

Chapter 5 A Hard Look at the Options Ahead: The Reality of the Changing Workplace 97

Chapter 6 Trading Up: Making the Organization You Work for Work for You 125

Chapter 7 Branching Out: Alternative Workplaces and Portfolio Careers 163

Chapter 8 The NeXt Generation Leader: Why You're What We Need Now . . . and How 187

Notes *217*

Index *231*

About the Author *237*

ACKNOWLEDGMENTS

Above all, my thanks go to every member of Generation X who took the time to talk with me, argue with me, write to me, post responses to my blog posts, or otherwise share your perspectives and ideas. Not all of you were supportive, but you all made me think—hard—about what, if anything, I could say that would be useful. I've done my best.

I found when I was writing this book that, in many instances, you really said it best. You'll see that I've left many points in your own distinctive voices, rather than attempting to paraphrase in any way.

Your voices

Great article–spot on! We always have a chuckle at every article written about Gen Y's (it's funny because it's true), so it's great to finally see an article acknowledge the undervalued Gen X'er . . . I'd offer a few ideas for your book, but then wouldn't *that* be typical of a Gen X'er–do the work, let the recognition go elsewhere! Great article–thanks!

The names of all those whose voices are included in the book are listed in the Notes section; my thanks to you and to the hundreds of others whose comments I just couldn't squeeze in. Special thanks go to X'ers Jean Ayers, Mike Dover, Joe Grochowski, Esteban Herrera, Beth Hilbing, Eric Kimble, Steven Kramer, Erinn McMahon, Rory Madden, and Becky Minard, who allowed me to tell their stories in detail. And to almost-X'er

Paul Michelman, my editor at HBP Digital, whose enthusiasm for this project has spurred many of the questions I've tried to wrestle with in these pages.

The research for *What's Next?* stretches back over six years of work and reflects the contributions of many colleagues. Bob Morison and Ken Dychtwald were lead partners in the original work. Tim Bevins and Maggie Hentschel conducted research specifically for this book. Tom Casey and Margaret Schweer made important contributions. Matt DeGreeff and Jason Siedel's comments on the early manuscript were enormously helpful. Thanks to you all.

Warm thanks go to the wonderful team at Harvard Business Publishing. I'm not sure I'd like to write three books in three years again anytime soon, but working with you all has been a great pleasure. Special thanks to my editors: Jacqueline Murphy, editorial director; Ania Wieckowski, assistant editor; and Monica Jainschigg, developmental editor. The broader HBP community has universally supported and engaged in this work: Angelia Herrin and Julie Devoll from its initiation, as well as the creative teams in HBP Corporate Learning who developed the ideas into learning tools; at HBP Digital who facilitated the conversations with many of you; and at *Harvard Business Review* as we expanded and explored some of the more important concepts of midcareer life and the changing workplace.

David, Kate, and all my friends, both two- and four-footed, at Black Brook Farm, have been a constant source of encouragement and support.

Tom, as always, I couldn't have done it without you.

INTRODUCTION

No doubt about it—the workplace has posed some special challenges for Generation X.

The demographic numbers and the economy have been stacked against you. As *Fortune* noted in 1985, "These pioneers of the baby-bust generation are finding life on the career frontier harsher than ever . . . they're snarled in a demographic traffic jam . . . stuck behind all those surplus graduates of the past decade."[1] The economy went into recession in 1991, and, just when some of you were gaining momentum, the bursting of the dot-com bubble wiped out $5 trillion in the market value of technology companies from March 2000 to October 2002.

And here you are. Fortyish, or soon to be. Some of you have made it to the top. Others have made it to where you think you want to be. Still others are still working up, heading out, or feeling frustrated about finding work that works for you.

This book shows you the options for *what's next* and how to get there by taking advantage of the attributes unique to your generation. While building the background for this advice, this book acknowledges, in your own words, the feelings many of you share and the common places you find yourselves as a generation. It celebrates your individuality and personal preferences. But more than anything, this book points to the practical implications of both. Because I've been warned:

Your voices

One word of advice: this book had better be *heavy* on actual content and *good practical advice*, and low on your typical Boomer touchy-feely bandwagony, fad "cheese-moving" pop psychology. If I see chapters on "Embracing Change," I'm going to vomit.

Got it.

This is the third book I've written to a generation, each of which faces unique challenges and brings specific strengths to today's workplace. A combination of the best from each is required for the challenging years ahead. My message to Boomers, even before the economic downturn, was to find ways to keep working; turn over the reins of leadership but find other ways to be productive contributors during the decades ahead: *Retire Retirement*. And my message to Y's was also practical; find ways to blend their strengths with the reality of what they'll find in the corporate world: get *Plugged In*.

And Gen X? Most of you plan to continue working for at least another couple of decades. Your challenge now is one of *how* to work, how to make sure the work you're doing is meaningful and rewarding against whatever criteria you use to measure success—if necessary, how to recalibrate midstream. These are critical questions for X'ers now. It's the right time in your life to start making these decisions and the generations that surround you—the Boomers and the Y's—are going to be competing for the same opportunities. You are in the middle of your lives, your careers, and the workforce: you are wedged between two huge generations that are each, in their own ways, taking up a little too much of your room.

Many of you have achieved a number of your initial goals and reached a comfortable self-sufficiency. But what are your next steps? You need to understand your options and weigh them appropriately, not just plod up the corporate ladder. Some of you are still wrestling with finding the career you want and are beginning to reframe your goals entirely. How do you reset your sights for the next stretch? And finally, there are many of you who feel you haven't yet hit your stride in the career that you *have* chosen: what's next for you? You may know what you want, but you just need some advice about how to get it.

One critical and timely consideration is how to maximize what have traditionally been peak career years to your full advantage, given today's turbulent economy. From a financial earnings perspective, the years between forty-five and fifty-four are when individuals typically reach maximum earnings. And the thirty-five to forty-four cohort, which most of you are in, ranks a close second, taking home only an average of 10 percent less than forty-five- to fifty-four-year-olds.[2] The way you spend the next decade of your life will have a powerful impact on your long-term financial stability and achievement of other work-related goals.

Most of you are working in large organizations that are themselves changing and, in many cases, struggling to adapt to global competition, new ways of operating, and challenging conditions. The economic downturn has hit your generation particularly hard. How can you maintain your balance during difficult times and leverage your contributions to create work opportunities that better match your personal definitions of success?

Some of you are considering entrepreneurship or other independent work arrangements. What does that mean for you? How can you increase your chances of success?

And it's not just about you, as you know. You are moving into a time in your lives when responsibility for others becomes a dominant theme. In the work sphere, whether in big companies or small, you are moving into senior leadership roles at a time when the challenge of leadership is changing, driven in part by new options and in large part by you and your sensibilities. What capabilities will you need to create the types of organizations you want to be part of and will be proud to leave behind? Beyond business, the decisions you make over the period ahead will have a powerful impact on your family, your personal satisfaction, and the larger society—on public policy decisions, business directions, and social welfare.

This book is an invitation to reflect on how your particular point in history has influenced who and where you are today, to think about your personal preferences in the context of the shared characteristics of your generation. And it's about how you want to invest the next phase of your life—what your priorities will be, where you will focus your time and energies.

For the past five years, I've been conducting research specifically on the role work plays in people's lives and the reasons different generations often appear to think and act in conflicting ways. Much of my focus has been on how work and the workforce are changing. I have had the opportunity to talk with many of you. The perspectives you've shared about your goals and preferences are reflected in this book, and your voices appear throughout. My colleagues and I have conducted large surveys to capture views from around the world. And I've had your help in shaping the conclusions from this research, through your comments during workshops and speeches and your thoughtful responses to my weekly blog.[3]

I have also worked with major global corporations for thirty years, helping them improve their business strategies and operational approaches. This experience forms the basis for my discussion of how organizations work, how they are evolving, and how you can succeed in these environments. Some of what I'll share will tap into my research and that of my colleagues on the ways globalization, new technologies, and changing employee values are reshaping the workplace.

Here's what this book includes.

Chapters 1 and 2 are about you as a generation, as teens and today. And chapter 3 is about *them*—the other four generations who share your lives, both at work and at home. I'll cover pivotal formative events, demographic influences, and relationships between the generations. And although generalizations are unavoidable in this broad-brush picture, my goal is not to stereotype but to suggest how legitimate it is for us each to bring different perspectives to the table. We are individuals because we are shaped by unique influences: our socioeconomic background, race, nationality, parents' views, upbringing, and other factors. Nonetheless, the individuals who share a common point in history—in other words, members of the same generation—develop similar conceptual maps or ways of viewing the world. It's a powerful point to explore and one that can help us relate to each other with more humor and tolerance. Understanding what we have in common also provides a context for understanding what is unique about each individual.

Chapters 4 through 8 provide an in-depth look at the changing workplace and its evolving opportunities. These chapters include tools to help you evaluate your next steps and questions that create a framework for considering options in a coherent way. I hope they meet your challenge for practical advice. Chapter 4 sets the stage with frameworks for exploring the characteristics of work that engages you. These exercises can help you evaluate your career up to this point and to shape the path going forward. Chapter 5 discusses the changing workplace and where the future jobs are. Chapter 6 offers practical advice for achieving more engagement and success—as you define it—within an organization. Chapter 7 asks you to consider if the entrepreneurial route might be for you and discusses strategies for a variety of alternative arrangements. Chapter 8 takes up the topic of you as a leader going forward and lays out what I think are the five most important responsibilities of tomorrow's leaders.

This book is above all an invitation to reflect on what you will do next. I hope reading it will help you feel more confident of your options and more comfortable in your choices. I hope you find some new possibilities and specific thoughts on how to achieve them.

You'll find that my point of view is fundamentally optimistic. You are at a point of enormous potential for both personal happiness and positive contributions to the world around you. There are great opportunities ahead.

This is a book for you.

Part I

You as a Generation

CHAPTER ONE

Shaping Generation X

Your Teen Years

Nobody likes to be pigeonholed. But there's a reason you're called *Generation* X, broad as that reason may be. By definition, a generation is a group a people who, based on their age, share not only a chronological location in history but also *the experiences that accompany it*. These common experiences, in turn, prompt the formation of shared beliefs and behaviors.

Many of our most powerful and lasting beliefs are formed when we are teenagers, when we first shift our focus from tangible objects and begin to wrestle with the values and ideas in the world around us. What we see and hear—and the conclusions we draw—influence for our lifetimes what we value, how we measure success, whom we trust, and the priorities we set for our own lives, including the role work will play within it.

This way of looking at the development of generational characteristics is based on the work of Swiss biologist and psychologist Jean Piaget. In his highly influential research on child development, Piaget concluded that children build cognitive structures—mental maps—to help make sense of their conceptual experiences when they are young teens. Piaget also concluded that it is primarily *new* experiences that alter the developing child's cognitive structure, rather than those that are perceived as having "always" been true.[1] So it's logical that each generation would form its own unique impressions and therefore, to some extent, operate under a different set of rules: each would have experienced a very different world when they were teens. These coming-of-age contrasts influence each generation's attitudes toward the world, toward work, and toward each other.

Of course, the commonalities are far from the whole story. Each one of you also had *unique* teen experiences, depending on the country you were living in, your family's socioeconomic background, your parents' philosophies, and a host of other factors. But the prominent events you *share* are what give your generation its defining characteristics.[2]

Those who write about your generation generally agree on some common traits, and the implications and tone are often pretty dark.

Douglas Coupland's novel, *Generation X: Tales for an Accelerated Culture,* provided the first portrait of your generation and popularized the name most commonly used in North America. A Canadian author, Coupland profiled a group of "underemployed, overeducated, intensely private and unpredictable" twenty-somethings who have "nowhere to direct their anger, no one to assuage their fears and no culture to replace their anomie."[3]

In *The Fourth Turning* and *Generations,* William Strauss and Neil Howe portray Generation X as:

> *brazen free agents, lending their pragmatism and independence to an era of growing social turmoil. [They] come of age in a society strong in choices and judgments but weak in structure, guidance, or any sense of collective mission for young adults. Lacking a generation core, they are defined by their very social and cultural divergence. Aware that elder leaders don't expect much from them as a group, they feel little collective mission or power. Yet their accelerated contact with the real world gives*

> *them strong survival skills and expectations of personal success . . .*[4] *[They] typically distrust institutions and authority; are alienated by elder criticism; become skeptical and learn to rely on instinct and experience rather than principle; might do things or seem to do things just for the hell of it; and generally make their own way rather than follow established patterns. Hearing others declare everything too complex for yes-or-no answers, [they] struggle to filter out noise, cut through rhetoric, and isolate the handful of practical truths that really matter.*[5]

The substance of these characterizations captures important realities for Generation X: many of you were and perhaps still are underemployed, you do lean toward being independent free agents, and, as Jon Stewart and other commentators attest, you have a real gift for cutting through rhetoric. But I am uncomfortable with an implication that your common characteristics are largely negative. These characteristics also translate into a terrifically useful set of traits—many that are particularly valuable in our current economic climate—and are rarely captured in most commentaries on your generation.

- Your accelerated contact with the real world has made you resourceful and hardworking. You meet your commitments and take employability seriously.
- Your distrust of institutions has prompted you to value self-reliance and to develop strong survival skills and the ability to handle whatever comes your way with resilience. You maintain a well-nurtured portfolio of options and networks.
- A sense of alienation from your immediate surroundings, coupled with rapidly expanding technology, has allowed you to look outward in ways no generation before could or did. You operate comfortably in today's world—global and digital. Many of you are avid users of collaborative technology in your personal lives. You work well in multicultural settings.

- Your preference for "alternative" and early experience in making your own way left you inclined to innovate. You tend to look for a different way forward.
- Free agency has led you to one of your strongest arenas of financial success as a generation—your entrepreneurial achievements.
- Your skepticism and ability to isolate practical truths have resulted in rich humor and incisive perspective.
- Your childhood made you fiercely dedicated to being good parents, prompting you to raise important questions about the way we all balance work with commitments beyond the corporation.
- Your pragmatism has given you practical and value-oriented sensibilities that, I believe, will help you serve as effective stewards of both today's organizations and tomorrow's world.

This chapter is about how you got to be the way you are. (Chapter 2 will discuss how these traits have played out in your life thus far.)

Generation X—A Brief (Demographic) Definition

It's hard to agree on Generation X's birth years. Most commonly, your generation is described as those born between 1965 and 1979, a framework tied to the "baby bust" pattern of birth rates that followed the preceding "baby boom"; 1965 was the year when U.S. birth rates plummeted, dropping from 4.3 million births at the peak of the boom in 1959 to only 3.8 million in 1965, and 3.1 million in 1973 at the trough of the bust (see figure 1-1).

However, many who were born between 1961 and 1964 prefer to be considered X'ers. They feel more aligned with Gen X values and claim little in common with the Boomer cohort. Barack Obama falls in this swing group, as do many of the early Gen X voices, including Douglas Coupland and Richard Linklater, director of the iconoclastic X'er movie, *Slacker*; all were born in 1961.[6]

FIGURE 1-1

The baby bust

THE YEARS OF LOW BIRTHS, 1965–1979

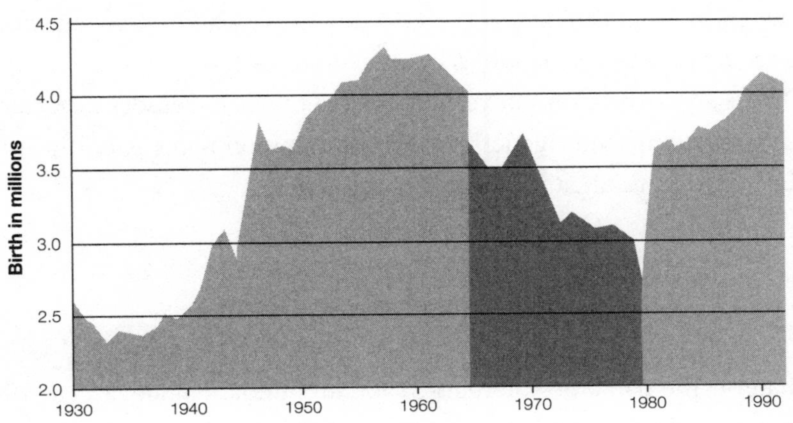

Source: U.S. Census Bureau International Data Base.

For purposes of this book, when I provide statistics, I will generally include those people born from 1965 to 1979 (or 1980, since many statistics are available only in five-year increments), although I'm increasingly persuaded that those born in the early 1960s share many, if not most, X'er sentiments.

Although the name *X* has stuck with you in North America, most countries around the world also have specific names for your generation,

Generation X

Born: 1965 (or 1961) to 1979

Formative teen years: 1980s and early 1990s

Age in 2009: twenty-nine to forty-three (or forty-eight) years old many of which reflect a sense of disenchantment or disenfranchisement, including *Génération Bof* ("whatever") in France; the *Burnt Generation* in Iran, representing those most negatively affected by the political and social consequences of the 1979 revolution; and the *Crisis Generation* in some Latin American countries, reflecting those who came of age during the recurring financial troubles in the region.

Some argue that X is, above all, a state of mind that eludes neat categorization. Perhaps your generation's most common name is oddly appropriate, since *X* is, after all, the unknown quantity.

The Temper of the Times

Whatever the name or boundaries, you are fundamentally a post-1980s generation. Generation X'ers were teens in the 1980s and 1990s, shaped by times marked with uncertainty and social change.

Your voices

What seems to have defined Gen X is the ill-defined threat. We had the Cold War, with its constant threat of nuclear holocaust. We had the [space shuttle] *Challenger* disaster, the start of the AIDS epidemic, and a president who was almost assassinated. We lived through a ton of divorces and moms entering the workforce. We became latchkey kids. We had reduce, reuse, recycle, and the first major energy crisis.[7]

A pretty fair summary of the events that characterized many of your teen years.

The Economy and Adult Employment

During your teen years, economies throughout much of the world were stagnant. Latin American countries were experiencing persistent financial crises. Economic stagnation was prevalent in Europe and the United States. President Ford had Americans sport "Whip Inflation Now" buttons as the economy struggled through the doldrums.

As teens, you witnessed a significant increase in adult unemployment when reengineering and other corporate restructuring dramatically revamped the concept of lifetime employment. The psychological contracts between employers and employees established through the 1960s and 1970s were ripped apart by the large-scale layoffs that accompanied the process redesign and downsizing initiatives of the 1980s and 1990s. Most X'ers who grew up in the United States knew at least one adult who was laid off from a job that was supposed to last until retirement. It may not have been your parent—perhaps it was a neighbor or a friend's parent—but watching the adults in your lives being laid off from corporations that they had depended on for a lifetime commitment is perhaps one of the most widely shared experiences of your generation. Mistrust of corporate commitments is an almost universally held view among X'ers.

Political Events

The ominous threat of the Cold War both came to the fore and ended when you were teens. Many of the most prominent global political events implied a promising future: Gorbachev began *glasnost* in 1985; the Berlin Wall fell in 1989; and, in 1991, Czechoslovakia's Velvet Revolution signaled the fall of Communism and the Soviet Union dissolved. Many older X'ers were deeply committed to working for these changes.

Although important local conflicts continued throughout the world, their impact on most teens in the United States, in particular, was relatively slight. The boycott of the 1980 Summer Olympics in Moscow made visible the Soviet war in Afghanistan. The first Gulf War occurred for one intense month in early 1991, with dramatic live coverage. But, with these exceptions, for most of your teen years, you did not spend your evenings, as Boomers did, watching televised war.

And yet you were surrounded by signs of shortcomings and ambiguity. Although the conflict in Vietnam had ended when you were children, the United States withdrew from Vietnam without having achieved any discernable objective, leaving many Americans angry and bewildered.[8] Throughout your childhood and adolescence, belief in the integrity of government eroded, from the illegal misdeeds of the Nixon White House, the Watergate hearings, and Nixon's subsequent resignation in 1974 to the moral misdeeds of the Clinton years, culminating in the Monica Lewinski scandal and the Clinton impeachment hearings in 1998. Most weeknights, the national news led with negative stories about politicians or government policy.[9] The leaders in your lives were not living up to a high standard, and a general unease around adult behavior became part of the Gen X teen experience.

Science and Technology

Your teen years also had a flavor of a "brave new world" of progress in science and technology. In some cases, the advances of technology were offset by spectacular failure or heated moral debate:

- The first "test-tube baby" was born in 1978.
- The meltdown in the Three Mile Island nuclear plant occurred in 1979.
- Tylenol tampering created widespread public fear in 1982.
- The Chernobyl nuclear energy plant exploded in 1986.
- The space shuttle *Challenger* blew up in 1986.
- Scientists cloned a sheep in 1997.
- *Pathfinder* sent photos of Mars in 1997.

The *Challenger* incident had a particular impact on many of you. Because a schoolteacher, the first civilian passenger, was a member of the crew, the launch was a major celebration in U.S. schools. Classes were recessed to allow students to watch the launch and, as a result, experience the ensuing disaster firsthand.

Your voices

The *Challenger* disaster probably had the largest single-event impact on my core beliefs. It was the first major U.S. screwup (of which I was aware) and it decimated my confidence in my country . . . At some point that disillusionment spread to corporate America. Expect nothing and you won't be disappointed. Yet I still believe that I may give nothing less than my best to my employer and country. The change, then, was that I learned to expect nothing in return.

Throughout your lives, the crescendo of information technology and its impact on all our lives have been steadily increasing. You were children when Bill Gates and Paul Allen started Microsoft in 1975 and just entering your teens as the Apple II became the first mass-marketed personal computer in 1977. Computers appeared in schools, and you learned to use them easily as new capabilities and applications developed. The Internet was in its infancy when you were in yours and grew dramatically throughout your teen and early adult years (see figure 1-2).

FIGURE 1-2

Growth in Internet users

INTERNET USAGE GROWTH, 1970–2006

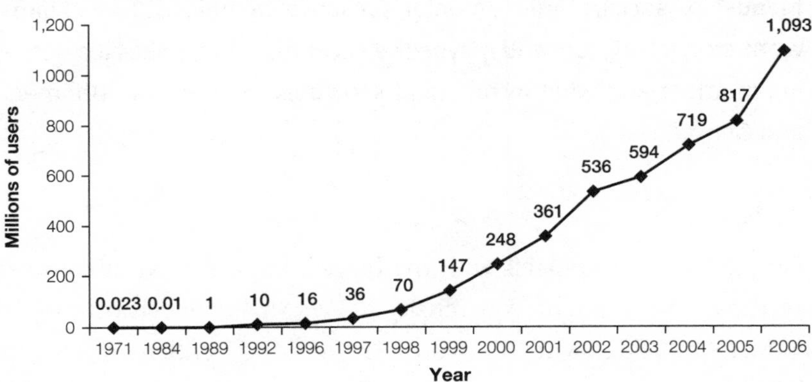

Source: www.internetworldstats.com.

Before there were computers in your homes, most of you learned to play video games, the early versions of which came out when you were children; *Space Invaders, Pong,* and *Pac-Man* were among the vanguard.[10] The mores of these games may have provided an imprint for some adult X behaviors: when things went wrong in these early games, the only solution was to reboot, to start over. For many X'ers today, starting over—moving on—is a not-uncommon response to roadblocks.

For many of you, these pre-Internet years, and even the pre-video-game years, are most memorable—and the ones to which you attribute much of your generation's creativity and tight friendships.

Your voices

If I was to pick one defining moment, it was when I was inducted as a young teen into the world of *Dungeons and Dragons*. Before mainstream computers, before mobiles, before the Internet . . . we became spellbound, living vicariously through our characters . . . The creativity and innovation generated at one session could very possibly, in my humble opinion, power a corporate board with Big Think Strategies for a year! I feel blessed that I had that opportunity to incubate in such a safe and supportive environment . . . It was the combination of friendship, social/physical/mental presence, a unified goal, teamwork, storytelling, fun, and maybe the sugar rush that makes it a defining moment and what in my mind separates me from the Boomers and Gen Y.

Perhaps the technologies with the biggest impact on your teen years were those that brought you music: MTV (Music Television) and the Walkman. In 1981, with the words "Ladies and gentlemen, rock and roll!" and a crunching guitar riff playing over a montage of the *Apollo* 11 moon landing, MTV launched.

Your voices

What do I remember as a teen? Without a doubt, the birth of MTV. Can't all X'ers in the U.S. remember exactly what they were doing when "Video Killed the Radio Star" came on for the first time? And, while technology was in its infancy stage, I bet most X'ers can also remember exactly when they got their first Sony Walkman.

These technologies amplified the impact of your music and helped shape your generation's perspectives on the world.

The Arts

MTV served as the stage for one of your generation's most distinctive identities—alternative rock. In 1991, Nirvana's "Smells Like Teen Spirit" and the band's lead singer Kurt Cobain invigorated X'er teens. Throughout the 1990s, you found voice—a deliberate, at times ferocious, positioning outside the mainstream into the "alternative" world. Cobain's suicide in 1993 was a major heartbreak for many in your generation, although the alternative movement continued on with hits like Radiohead's "Creep," released in 1992, and Beck's "Loser" in 1994, two of the defining songs of the nineties.

Unlike Boomers, who more or less coalesced around rock and roll, your music reflected your wide range of cultural sensibilities—from the anarchy and nihilism of punk in the late seventies and early eighties, to the pure hedonism of eighties hair bands' glam metal, to the ironic and painful self-awareness of nineties grunge.

The "X sensibility" extended into the movies throughout the 1990s. Young directors explored a disappointing youth economy (*Clerks, Reality Bites*) and a life that seemed to lead nowhere (*Slacker, Singles*). The films you watched as teens were filled with alienation (*sex, lies, and videotape*), exploitative sexuality (*Kids, My Own Private Idaho*), and remorseless violence (*Natural Born Killers, Pulp Fiction, Reservoir Dogs*). *Wall Street* reflected the "greed is good" philosophy of the eighties "me decade" and the rise of the Yuppies.

During your childhood and early teen years, production of happy movies *for* kids plummeted. The proportion of G-rated films fell from 41 percent of all movies to only 13 percent through the 1970s and 1980s. Disney laid off cartoonists for the first time in its history.[11] Creative-kid movies were replaced with a new genre featuring unwanted, unlikable, or simply horrifying children. *Rosemary's Baby,* about a woman pregnant with Satan's child, signaled the beginning of a twenty-year period of bad-kid movies (*The Exorcist, The Omen, Halloween*).[12]

Global Awareness and Social Activism

In addition to the music it popularized, MTV did something else for your generation: it gave you a perspective that extended beyond music and beyond national boundaries. X'ers became the first generation of youth to develop a global perspective and empathy, often through the televised events that raised funds for and awareness about AIDS (first identified in 1981), apartheid (which ended in South Africa in 1993), world famine, and a host of other global issues.

Your voices

We too had our "causes" that brought light to world issues—like Band Aid, Live Aid, Farm Aid, and Hands Across America. These gave birth to new goodwill ambassadors like Bono, Madonna, and Sting. We were now looking at world issues in a much different light. I don't know that other generations ever cared about what went on with famine in Africa, apartheid, or how people actually lived in Communist countries.

MTV was not alone, of course. Cable brought a host of eye-opening channels directly into your homes, including CNN, HBO, and even Playboy, widening your window on the world in multiple dimensions.

Diversity issues were evolving rapidly during your teen years. Within your own generation, you are diverse in many dimensions. Racially, within the United States, 63 percent of you are non-Hispanic whites, 17 percent are Hispanic, 13 percent are black, and 6 percent are Asian. You are a point on the continuum of continuing racial diversity. Among the Boomers, 73 percent are non-Hispanic white, while among children under five, only 56 percent are.[13]

The civil rights movement had made significant strides toward abolishing racial discrimination by the time you were teens. Major legislation, including the Civil Rights Act of 1964, created a foundation of laws designed to protect the rights of African Americans and other minorities before most of you were born. For you, television played an important role in creating a broader base of understanding. *Roots,* based on the novel by Alex Haley and broadcast as a twelve-hour miniseries in 1977, is viewed by many as a turning point in mainstream America's ability to relate to the realities of African American history.

The women's rights movement was gaining momentum during your youth. Both the Equal Rights Amendment (ERA) and Title IX of the Education Amendments were passed by Congress in 1972. Title IX, which banned sex discrimination in schools, had a strong impact on your generation. As a result of Title IX, the enrollment of women in athletics programs and professional schools increased dramatically during your teen and early adult years.

Throughout the 1970s and particularly in the 1980s, women began entering the workforce in significant numbers. Eighty percent of Boomer women eventually chose to work outside the home at some point in their lives. On average, the percentage of women in the workforce during the time X'ers were teens rose from the mid-30 percent range to nearly 60 percent. For some of you, these women were your mothers; for others, the Boomers represented older siblings, neighbors, or other role models.

In 1984, one of the landmark events in the women's rights movement occurred: the nomination of Democrat Geraldine Ferraro as the first female vice presidential candidate of a major American political party. You are the first generation that grew up seeing women in strong leadership roles.

Concurrent with the women's rights movement, reproductive choice was at its peak during your teen years. The Supreme Court had established a woman's right to safe and legal abortion through *Roe* v. *Wade* in 1973. Abortion rates skyrocketed through the 1970s; in 1980, and in 1981 nearly one pregnancy in three was terminated. (Today, the comparable figure is 22 percent, or approximately one in five.)[14]

The gay rights movement also made significant strides when you were teens. The onset of the AIDS epidemic in the 1980s, in addition to being a personal and social tragedy of immense proportions, paradoxically strengthened the political arm of the gay movement. Although the Moral Majority political organization was formed in the 1979 in opposition to gay rights, among other issues, homosexual behavior was decriminalized in many states through the 1990s.

Bottom line: You grew up more tolerant of diversity—racial, gender, and sexual orientation—than any generation before.

Family and Friends

Some of the biggest changes during your generation's teen years were occurring on the domestic scene. X'ers lived through a significant shift in the social fabric—a rebalancing of the roles of friends and family, and a change in expectations of teen independence.

For those of you whose mothers stepped into the external world of work, their new responsibilities frequently left you on your own. There was little infrastructure or institutional support for working mothers in the 1980s—few day-care centers, no nanny networks or company-sponsored child care. As a result, many of you became part of the first wave of "latchkey kids."

The dynamic of working mothers and latchkey kids was intensified by a significant increase in divorce rates. Those of you who lived in the United States saw divorce rates among your parents' generation skyrocket from the

FIGURE 1-3

Growth in divorce rates

U.S. MARRIAGES ENDING IN DIVORCE

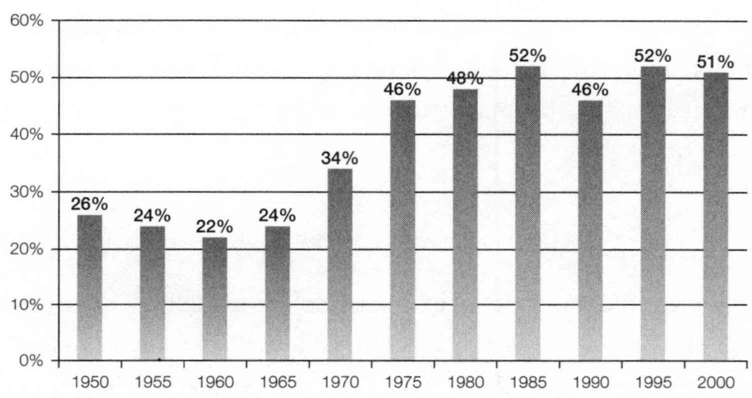

Source: National Center for Health Statistics 2000.

low 20 percent level when you were young to over 50 percent by the time you were teens (see figure 1-3). Divorce rapidly became a common occurrence among your classmates and friends, if not in your own family. You are four to five times more likely than Boomers to have experienced divorce.[15]

The growing number of single-parent homes intensified the likelihood that many of you spent your afternoons alone, taking care of yourselves and possibly your siblings, or hanging out with friends for support—a trend that films like *Ferris Bueller's Day Off* picked up, depicting kids as competent and independent.

And the lack of a strong family structure left many of you exposed to adult issues while you were still chronologically children. You grew up very fast.

Your voices

My adolescent years were spent not only watching my parents' marriage dissolve but my mother's transformation from housewife to working professional. It was an emotional roller coaster at the time.

Many of you formed deep relationships with the friends who were with you during the high school years. The popular television shows *Friends* and *Seinfeld,* both ensemble casts about groups of tightly knit friends, were based on you. You and your friends often passed the time in one of the new venues available to your generation, shopping malls. There, bored and cynical, you developed a jaded self-awareness from exposure to the omnipresent marketing messages.

Your voices

One thing we did have that generations before us didn't were malls. Malls gave us a place to hang out (with our friends of course, not family), we became major consumers since our social activities were directly associated with retail, and we put a much greater emphasis on our appearance.

Today, many of you say you continue to rely more on friends than you do on family and are often reluctant to relocate away from your established circle of close friends. The dual experience of caring for yourself as teens, but with support from your friends, accounts for a seeming paradox in your values: you are simultaneously both self-reliant and "tribal."

Strauss and Howe see your generation as a group of neglected teens who were left unprotected at a time of cultural convulsion and adult self-discovery:

> *Ask today's young adults how they were raised, and many will tell you that they raised themselves—that they made their own meals, washed their own clothes, decided for themselves whether to do homework or make money after school, and chose which parent to spend time with on weekends . . . They grew up . . . as free agents, looking forward to dealing and maneuvering their way through life's endless options . . . [X'ers]*

were denied a positive vision of the future—denied, indeed, any reassurance that their nation had any collective future at all.[16]

These events reinforced an impression that the adults in your lives—now the older generations in your workplace—were neither virtuous nor powerful, or in control of their own personal lives or of the larger world. For many in Generation X, parents were coordinators with limited voice or authority. As Strauss and Howe put it, "Instead of preventing danger or teaching by example, adults were more apt to hand out self-care guides that told kids about everything that might happen and how to handle it on their own."[17]

Your voices

Erinn was just turning thirty-nine when we spoke, a self-described "helicopter parent" to two children, and a respected professional within her firm.[18] *As a teen, Erinn was a latchkey kid.*

My friends and I never saw our parents. Because so many of our parents were working hard or divorced, they were nonexistent in our lives. My mother was never there; I'm not sure what it was she was doing.

We learned from a very early age that we needed to take care of ourselves. For example, I wouldn't have thought of asking my parents for help with homework. We had to depend on ourselves. We had to fend for ourselves. If we wanted something, we had to do it for ourselves.

We wanted to be excellent—not necessarily better than our friends—we weren't competitive—but we needed to be excellent. We were trying to get the attention of parents who were not there. We had to be the best in order to get approval from adults. It was necessary to be the best.

Your generation's shared characteristics, like those of all generations, stem from your early experiences—in your case, many of these involved critical institutions that *all* seemed to let you down. In the next chapter, I'll discuss the implications of Gen X traits for where you are today in the workplace and in your lives more broadly.

CHAPTER TWO

Taking Stock

Generation X Today

Every generation faces its own particular set of challenges based on the specific events it encounters along its unique path through history. Here's the bottom line for Gen X: at each point thus far, you've drawn a pretty short straw. Your timing—at least in the context of contemporary generations and through no fault of your own—could hardly have been worse. Not only did your childhood years coincide with social changes that significantly eroded trust and idealism, but during the early years of your adulthood, you have hit various economic landmarks at unfavorable points in the cycle.

- You have invested significant time and money in education and are today the most credentialed generation yet, but changes in the funding available for college education mean that yours came at a high personal cost.
- Many of you entered the workforce at a difficult time, queued up behind a generation of Boomers and competing for fewer jobs in a weak economy.

- Just as Boomers may be leaving the higher spots open to you, you are now being squeezed by queue-jumping Y's.
- You bought homes when they were at peak values, prices having been driven up by the large bulge of home-buying Boomers.
- You are entering leadership roles when the challenges you will face as leaders could hardly be more difficult.

Through it all, you've shown yourself as deeply committed to being excellent parents and have remained uncommonly loyal to your circle of friends. You have made unparalleled contributions to two related phenomena: innovation and humor. And here you are—with long life expectancies and many more years ahead, facing choices and challenges.

In later chapters, I'll explore options and strategies for what's next. But first, let's look in greater detail at where you are today.

A Slow Start: Weak Economy and Pipe-Clogging Boomers

The truth is, most X'ers' careers got off to a slow start, and many of you are still feeling the pain. You graduated when the economy was slow and Boomers had already grabbed most of the key jobs. As an article in a 1985 issue of *Fortune* said: "[T]hese pioneers of the baby-bust generation are finding life on the career frontier harsher than ever . . . they're snarled in a demographic traffic jam . . . stuck behind all those surplus graduates of the past decade."[1]

Unemployment hit 10.3 percent in 1983; college placement directors were saying it was the worst job market for college graduates since World War II. And there was depressing evidence of the employment market's competitiveness, as graduating tail-end Boomers and early X'ers struggled to find jobs: starting salaries of college graduates with a bachelor's degree in business declined by 8 percent, adjusted for inflation, in the ten years from the 1973–1974 recruiting season to 1983–1984.[2] By

1985, even many of the graduating seniors who had found jobs were deeply anxious about prospects for leading a comfortable upper-middle-class life.

The layoffs of the late eighties and early nineties didn't just affect your parents; they also altered the job market for you and pushed college grads into more transactional jobs. The stock market crashed in 1987. Many of you were forced to settle for what Douglas Coupland termed a *McJob*: "A low-pay, low-prestige, low-dignity, low-benefit, no-future job in the service sector. Frequently considered a satisfying career choice by people who have never held one."[3]

Your voices

When I got out of college in the early 1990s, the job market was terrible. X'ers had to fight for entry-level positions with a horde of "downsized" Boomers who had years of experience and were so in debt that they desperately needed any position, even if it was entry level.

I graduated college in 1989 and entered a very tight job market. After three months of interviewing, I had a choice of a $13,500 per year opportunity as a "writer" (I'm not a writer) and a $21,000 per year opportunity in a nonexempt role with a consulting firm. I took the nonexempt job and got in line behind an army of more experienced and more self-promoting Baby Boomers. The economy entered a recession eight months afterwards, and my company instituted a hiring freeze. So for several years, I remained in the junior ranks. Over time, I worked my way up to a partner position in the organization, taking about 30 percent more time to attain that level as my predecessors.

As one journalist put it, "Increasingly, younger workers are finding that no matter how many hours they put in or how much their bosses rave about their work, they're just plain stuck. An entire generation is bumping against something no amount of youthful vigor can match. Generation X, it would seem, is in danger of turning into the Prince Charles of the American workforce: perpetual heirs apparent awaiting the keys to the kingdom."[4]

Your voices

In the workplace, the X'ers' high work ethic is appreciated by our bosses (the Boomers), and to some extent it is what has allowed us to get to where we currently are, in "almost top management." It is definitely something we all should be proud of, but . . . we've been in "almost" mode for a long time.

It's Hell in the Hallways

Let's acknowledge that, for many X'ers, work to this point has been far from a fulfilling aspect of your life, in part because of the colleagues you've encountered there, in the hallways. You are sandwiched in between two large generations, both of which, to some extent, make many of you uncomfortable. Boomers seem to have already taken the good jobs, benefited from the good economy, purchased the good real estate, and—it often seems—had all the good breaks.

Granted, not all of you have had negative experiences with the Boomers in your life. Many have been guides and mentors, displaying hard work habits, corporate survival skills, and even some 1960s iconoclasm that have attracted and inspired you in the workplace. But many of you have had your problems with this generation and are divided from them not only because of their natural generational advantages, but because of the way they use their advantages to block X'ers.

Your voices

Gen X'ers have grown to dislike their interactions with Boomers. They've been spoiled all their life, are some of the most power-hungry and class-oriented people ever produced in America. X'ers leave corporations because there's a "Boomer ceiling" put firmly in place by Boomers who always have to get theirs but don't know how to share.

My fundamental concern with these Boomers has been their lack of faith and trust in the X generation. This is evident in the difficulty many X'ers seem to have in finding and holding mentors, in sustaining a career growth path at a velocity one would expect to see, lack of merit/performance-based career growth, and in finding "satisfaction" in the workplace. Throw in the parenting pressure and the associated financial pressures of raising and educating those kids, and you quickly develop a survivalist mind-set.

And now you have been joined in the workplace by Generation Y. Some X'ers find Y's threatening; many find them annoying. In our conversations, some of you have worried about Y's greater technical sophistication and high, fresh energy. Many of you have been counting the days until the Boomers clear out of the workplace, but just as that is beginning, Y's present a new wave of competition.

Your voices

I (a Gen X'er) think of it as being a second-string quarterback to the Boomers when the job opportunities were not there. Then, just before the first-string guy retires, they draft a promising youth who garners all the accolades and attention.

The new techie jobs are going to Y's who leapfrog over X'ers . . . Sigh.

Naturally, your individual opinions on Y's differ, with some of you (from my observation, often the younger among you, those more on the cusp) enjoying their presence in the workforce.

Your voices

My wife manages a fifteen-person team with three Y's, five Boomers, and six X'ers. She loves her Y's. Her exact words were "if I could trade my entire team for Y's, I would." She continues, "They are the most proactive, they need the least direction, and they have the best communication skills. They also think more like I do." For the record, she's thirty-three.[5]

To complicate matters further for many of you, these two generations—Boomers and Y's, each of whom can be annoying on their own—are crazy about each other. There is a near-zero generation gap between members of Generation Y and Boomers in the workplace, as I'll discuss in chapter 3. X'ers are, in fact, surrounded by a love fest and not feeling the love.

Your voices

I'm forty and, up until a few years ago, I was working as a managing editor for entertainment Web sites and magazines. The old guard was absolutely in love with Gen Y in both my last two jobs, and I definitely felt out of the loop.

I feel sandwiched in between the two demographic classes. It's as if the Boomers still don't take us seriously, and the Gen Y's look down at us as being too old.

That's how it *feels* for many of you. Let's look at how it plays out in the facts.

Your Balance Sheet at Halftime

A quick glance at the statistics would portray a generation that actually has been highly successful in the workplace by the conventional metric of money and the standard of living it can buy. The median incomes of Gen X *households* are higher than the national median and higher than they were for comparable age groups in 1990, adjusted for inflation.

However, a per person, rather than per household, view reveals that the positive uptick for your generation has come about because more of you have been working or, more specifically, because the women as well as the men of your generation are in the labor force. Today more than 80 percent of all Gen X'ers work.[6] You participate at rates that are higher overall than those of other generations. Two-thirds of all Gen X couples are dual-income earners.[7]

And the majority of you work full time. Of those of you between twenty-five and forty-four years old in 2005, only 4 to 6 percent of working men and 19 to 20 percent of working women worked part time.[8] "Full time" for Gen X employees today represents more paid and unpaid hours per week than it did for your age counterparts in 1977.[9]

Bottom line: you've achieved higher per household incomes than ever before, but you've done it by working—a lot.

And, unfortunately, despite higher average household incomes, many members of Generation X are in a precarious financial position today, due in large part to the timing of your major life events within recent economic cycles.

Expensive Education and High Debt

Many of you entered adult life with high levels of college-related debt. You began your college years just as the U.S. government made significant cuts in educational grants, shifting the burden of funding a college education toward loans throughout the 1980s. In 1993, borrowing limits on student loans were raised and unsubsidized loans were made available for middle-income students, making more students eligible for educational debt and increasing your generation's overall debt burden.

On the positive side, a greater percentage of your generation entered into postsecondary education of all kinds.[10] Today, you are the best-educated generation in history. But the median debt held by Gen X–headed households is double that held by Boomers at a comparable age.[11]

Your voices

As for this Gen X'er, I love my job, but I was "enjoying" the strong economy in college and law school because "Get a good (which meant a graduate degree of some sort) education and you'll be set" was the lie we were told. Now, I can't pay my $100,000 student loans and live in a one-bedroom apartment (because who can—or wants to—get a home loan these days?), driving the car that I bought in law school. I'm set alright . . . set to be in debt the rest of my life . . .

Costly Home Ownership

You have almost certainly been hit harder by the decline in housing prices and ensuing mortgage crisis of 2008 than any other generation. Your higher incomes, coupled with the significantly more flexible mortgage requirements of the past decade, enabled a high percentage of you to buy homes and to buy them sooner than Boomers did.[12] Today, the majority of Gen X'ers are homeowners.[13]

But you're paying a high price for that now. Many X'ers purchased homes at the top of the housing market, after prices had been driven up by the larger group of home-buying Boomers that preceded you. During the first half of this decade, the combination of still-increasing housing prices and your trade-ups to costlier homes caused the median value of homes owned by those in the thirty-five to forty-four age cohort to rise by 20 percent. Gen X'ers today on average own the most expensive homes in the country.[14] Unfortunately, during the same period, the amount of your generation's home-secured debt rose even faster, by nearly 30 percent.[15]

Low Net Worth

Even before the 2008 mortgage crisis, you were the first contemporary generation to have lower net worth than preceding generations did at the same age, thanks to a drop in the price of your homes and pre-2008 losses of your assets in the stock market. As a generation, your net worth, defined as the amount remaining after all your debts are subtracted from all your assets, has fallen over the past decade and is substantially lower than the net worth of Boomers or Traditionalists at a comparable age, when adjusted for inflation.[16] Between 2000 and 2004, the median net worth for householders aged thirty-five to forty-four fell by 16 percent. Yours was the only age group to experience a loss in net worth during these years.[17]

Your voices

We started off in a terrible economy; we hit our peak, so to speak, in a terrible economy. And we are going broke.

Growing Financial Commitments

The picture gets more worrisome. X'ers are in or are now entering the life stage associated with the heaviest spending. The late forties are when previous generations have increased their housing and child-rearing expenses before beginning to downsize in their fifties. For some of you, your commitments extend not only to housing and your children's education, but increasingly to caregiving for aging parents.

And this is the time when most individuals begin to think about saving for retirement in a serious way. Your generation has largely written off Social Security; polls show that most of you expect the system to go bankrupt before you see a dime in benefits.[18] According to a survey at the University of Colorado in 1996, Gen X'ers responded that they had a better chance of seeing a UFO in their lifetimes than a Social Security check.[19] Yet for many of you, significant saving, given the other demands on your income, is impossible. Those of you who had begun saving have almost certainly lost money this decade.

Even financial commitments that most would agree are urgent priorities are not possible for a significant proportion of your generation. Access to health insurance is a troubling financial issue for many X'ers. Today, approximately one in four of you has no health insurance. Most Americans obtain health insurance through their employers, but among twenty-five- to thirty-four-year-olds, only 61 percent had employment-based coverage in 2004.[20]

Your voices

I was laid off from a great career in 2001. Due to 9/11 and the great change in technology in my industry, salaries have gone down and I have not held a full-time position in seven years. I am back in school racking up student-loan and credit-card debt trying to prepare for a second career . . . I am living worse now than I was the year after I graduated. I was taught that I should choose a career I love and work hard and I would be rewarded. And yet, I am forty and I can't even afford health benefits or a cell phone. I have one full year of my master's and do not feel confident that I will find a good position. I wish you all the best of luck and hope you are faring better than me.

Of course, as with any average, there are exceptions to this portrait. Two-thirds of you have jobs that cover your health care, for example. Many of you have been highly successful in a corporate career and are now assuming leadership roles in major organizations. Some of you are dot-com or Wall Street millionaires, although even among those, there are many that speak to the struggles your generation has encountered along the way.

Your voices

I was part of the dot-com bust in the early part of this decade. I wasn't one of the success stories, and for as many success stories, there are a hundred stories like mine. I put all of my savings and energy into making a dot-com business, and it didn't work out. I've had to go through a rebuilding, like many other Gen X'ers. I've now had to navigate through a tough corporate environment not once, but several times.

Parents, Caregivers, Friends: Life Outside Work

For many of you, your own parenting pressures are at a peak. Generation X married later in life than any previous generation, and you've chosen to have children later, meaning that for many of you, even those in your forties today, you are still in the very active stage of rearing small children.

The median age of first marriages climbed steadily over the second half of the twentieth century and today rests around age 27 for men and age 25.5 for women in the United States.[21] The average is even higher in many other countries.[22]

In 2000, 40 percent of Gen X women and over 60 percent of Gen X men in the United States in the twenty-five to thirty-four age group had no children. This represents a sharp shift from the Boomer generation. In 1975, less than a quarter of all women in this age group were childless.[23]

But among X'ers with children, although you are having them later, a significant segment of you are having *more*. Between 1995 and 2000, the proportion of women having three or more children jumped from 11 percent to 18 percent.[24]

As I will discuss further in chapter 4, you are deeply committed to spending more time with your kids than your parents did or were able to spend with you, but juggling is getting more and more difficult.

Your voices

For a *huge* chunk (pretty much anyone in their thirties or forties with kids . . . and that's an awful lot of people), this is a *huge* issue. It wouldn't be if companies were more flexible about schedules, telecommuting, etc., but they all still seem to have the Boomer generation's attitude that you aren't really working unless you're doing it from nine to five, and doing it at your desk.

Throughout, many of you continue to be sustained by deep relationships with friends, particularly those who supported you through the high school years. San Francisco writer Ethan Watters, who coined the phrase "urban tribe" to describe X'ers' tight relationships, says: "These may be the people you turn to to discuss the absurdities of the day, share confidences, help each other define goals, fall in and out of love, and schlep couches and big-screen TVs from one apartment to the next."[25]

Your voices

Esteban is thirty-three, married, and a very successful professional. Born in Costa Rica, he moved to Boston when his parents did postgraduate work. There his family lived in a solidly middle-class suburb before returning to Costa Rica. Esteban graduated high school early at seventeen and returned to the Boston area to attend college at Babson.[26]

In our twenties, my closest friends and I all went various places as we started our careers—one to Japan, one to Europe, one to Latin

America—but we have wound up as five married couples living within a few miles of each other in a city that none of us grew up in.

Most of us met when we were in college . . . Babson, as a school, couldn't have been better for me. But it was difficult socially. There was a huge contingent of international students where you would have thought that I would have fit in, but they were all paying full tuition and had very different lifestyles from mine. I had to work sixty hours a week to pay my expenses. I was more like the Americans, but they didn't know how to relate to me, or me to them!

I found a small circle of close friends, mostly immigrants, all very hard workers. None of us had money, but we were all pretty talented at one thing. Thomas was from Poland and was the logical problem solver. Emma, who is also first-generation, and I were great writers. Lauren was a math geek. Dan was inspirational; he could resolve any conflict and keep our energy levels up. We did all the school projects together as a team during our junior and senior years and were extraordinarily competitive against other teams.

We had an interesting experience in our senior year. At the time, a job offer from Andersen Consulting was one of the most prestigious and sought-after options; every year they hired two men and two women from Babson. Out of our class of 400, 205 of us applied to work there. They did behavioral interviewing, testing attitudes. In the end, out of the 205 applicants, they ended up hiring Thomas, Emma, Lauren, and me. I don't think they knew that we were a team. But we all told similar stories.

Our other close friend Dan initially tried the entrepreneurial route, but later was also hired by Andersen. We all stayed various lengths of time at Andersen and made several other close friends who became part of our group there. Thomas and Dan remain part of my closest circle of friends; they're like my family.

Today most of my friends live in Dallas, in houses only a few miles apart. We wanted an urban setting, as opposed to the 'burbs—we make fun of suburbanites—but ended up in Dallas without any serious discussion. One of us was living there, then one by one, the rest of us just ended up moving there. Now it feels almost like an act of betrayal to move away.

We married outside of our original group, although some of us dated within the group at various times. I married someone I met when I was working in South America, a Brazilian. Her career defines her as much as mine defines me; she's analytical and very smart.

Some of us have kids; some of us don't. All who had kids had them later in life—within the last couple of years. I'm not opposed to children, but I have no immediate desire to have any.

We come from families with long-term marriages; of the five couples who live in Dallas, only one of the ten members is from a divorced family. And I think foreigners, Latinos in particular, need the physical proximity to family more. We latch on to friends tighter. My friends and I have built strong family-like bonds.

My mother calls us the global generation. The friends we consider "close" represent many nationalities and, despite a core that all live in Dallas, include individuals living in multiple countries around the world.

For many of you, your friends are your family, your community, and your closest source of support. Interestingly, criticism of Generation X often focuses on your lack of civic or social responsibility, as evidenced by your disinclination to join community organizations. As a generation, you tend not to attend church socials, join the League of Women Voters, or hang out at the Elks Club. Nor, as Robert Putnam wrote in his book *Bowling Alone*, do you join bowling leagues. Putnam says, "By virtually every conceivable measure, social capital has eroded steadily and sometimes dramatically over the past two generations . . . The quantitative evidence . . . is overwhelming."[27]

Putnam missed the role that your "tribes" play in creating your community and even in facilitating your work for social good.

Your voices

We have Wednesday wine nights. We also travel as a tribe quite a bit at least twice a year. Gyms and yoga studios are part of our nonwork interests and are also a good place to expand the tribe or join a new one. We have gourmet clubs, and we contribute to politicians and certain causes. Many of my closest friends go to church quite often. I think the networking institutions are evolving, not gone![28]

Distinctive Contributions: Innovation and Humor

Your achievements to this point are particularly notable in two closely related arenas. A number of years ago, I worked with colleagues to study people who were proven "innovators" to see if there were other personal characteristics that correlated with this ability. We found two: tolerance for a messy office . . . and the ability to tell a good joke. Tolerance for a messy office probably relates to an ability to work through ambiguity. A good joke requires starting a story in one direction, then adding an unexpected twist at the end. The essence of innovation is finding those unexpected twists. I don't know if Generation X is more tolerant of messes than other generations, but you do have both a track record for innovation and a wickedly funny sense of humor.

You grew up alongside the computer and the Internet and were the first generation to enter the workplace with these powerful tools. You have transformed and extended the technology in innovative ways. Appropriately, a generation of independent individualists has given us ways for people to express that individuality: Google, YouTube, Amazon, Second Life, PayPal, Wikipedia, and literally hundreds of other life-changing new ideas have all sprouted from innovative Gen X minds.

Your "alternative" point of view has made you a generation of astute observers and piercing commentators who are very, *very* funny. Your brand of humor—smart, irreverent, sarcastic, heavy on the irony—rules the comedy circuit today. No other generation has mastered "snark" as you have. From Jon Stewart's *The Daily Show*, Stephen Colbert's *The Colbert Report*, and *South Park*, we gain some of our clearest voices of reason and dissent. It's a voice you take to the workplace that gives you perspective and a way to sort through today's complex challenges. Gen X's humor could arguably be the single biggest thing that defines you culturally.

So, *What's Next, Gen X?*

What *is* next? Throughout the remainder of this book, I'll discuss how the values formed in your teen years and the reality of your adult experiences thus far combine to define what's next. I'll also look at the context for those options in terms of what other generations value and how the world of work is changing.

Whatever the options, you'll have a long time.

Long Life Expectancy

Although conventional wisdom might lead you to believe you're reaching some sort of midpoint, data on life expectancies would say that you're nowhere near that yet. Thanks to health care and other quality-of-life advances, life expectancies have shot up over the past century, almost doubling in most countries. Gerontologists believe that humans, at least those who live healthily, will soon have life spans of more than one hundred twenty years.[29]

A longer life expectancy will *not* prolong your years of being "old." For most, it will extend your period of an active "middle." Most of you will probably have something like sixty to eighty years of healthy, active, post-teen, pre-elderly, adult lifetime to build multiple careers, work in corporations, do something entrepreneurial, return to school to retool, contribute to your community, and enjoy your families. And, given that most X'ers are only ten to twenty years into this adult span, thinking in terms of fifty or sixty *more* years of productive time is not an unreasonable bet.

This long life expectancy affects you in radical ways. You need to look at the arc of your life very differently than your parents may have viewed theirs. As you consider what's next, you need to envision how you want to spend another fifty or sixty years, not another twenty. While I don't expect that you'll be working in a nine-to-five, five-days-a-week job for all that time, you will almost certainly live long enough that the idea of "retiring" into complete relaxation at age fifty, or even age seventy, will seem ridiculous and, for many of you, will be financially impossible.

On the positive side, you clearly have plenty of time to get work right if you're not in a good place yet. You have time to reposition yourself if that's what you want to do, to realign the trajectory you're on today or to plan for an entirely new set of activities down the road.

Moving the Milestones

As a consequence of longer life expectancies, all the conventional milestones of life are shifting upward. We've all heard about forty being the new thirty, but let's start even earlier. In many ways, thirty may be the new twenty.

Traditionally, progress toward adulthood has been measured with observable landmarks: marriage, financial independence, home ownership, and children. You are not only taking these steps later than previous generations did, but are also coming to them over a much wider time span, with much greater variation. Most X'ers don't reach these traditional markers until after age thirty.[30]

It's probably not a coincidence that many younger X'ers hesitate to characterize themselves as "adults." Only 70 percent of twenty-six- to thirty-five-year-olds answer an unambiguous yes when asked if they feel they have reached adulthood (see figure 2-1).

Does it matter? Is there any significance to reaching these various milestones in life? Certainly not from an extrinsic perspective: they don't measure your value or life success. But milestones ground us. And they can help you shape your own intrinsic view of yourselves to determine whether you are on track, "keeping up," or what that would even mean within your generation.

FIGURE 2-1

Do you feel that you have reached adulthood?

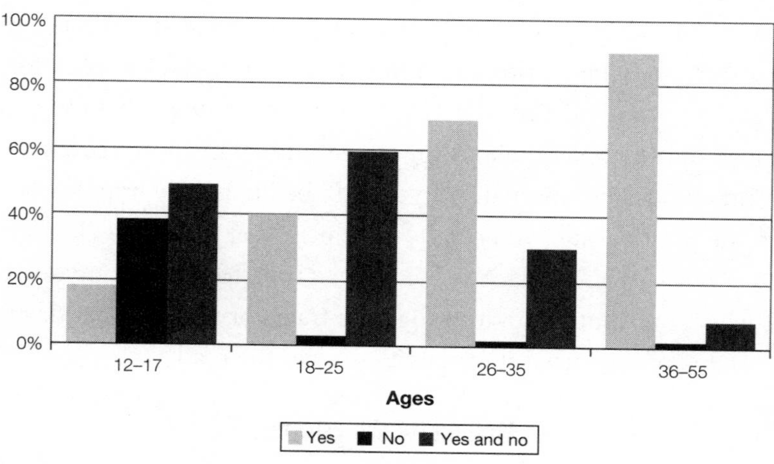

Source: Jeffrey Jensen Arnett, *Emerging Adulthood: The Winding Road from the Late Teens Through the Twenties* (New York, Oxford: Oxford University Press, 2004), 15.

In *Grown-ups: A Generation in Search of Adulthood,* Cheryl Merser suggests that all the postwar cohorts, beginning with the Boomers, have had to deal with an increasingly ambiguous transition to adulthood. Traditional markers made sense when people tended to do more or less the same things at more or less the same time.[31] But with your generation, synchronicity has largely disappeared. You each chose very different paths to get where you are today, in terms of the timing or extent of your education, your jobs and career, and your choices about marriage and child rearing.

The absence of a lockstep approach is positive in terms of increased individual latitude. The challenge is that all this variation can also be unsettling and leave individuals feeling a bit directionless. Without markers, it's easy to feel lost, to find yourself asking, "Have I done enough? Am I where I need to be?"

Sociologist James Cote points out that feeling confident in your identity means being able to place yourself securely on a continuum along the past, present, and future. If traditional markers no longer define the continuum, what benchmarks do we use instead?[32] How do we think about where we are at this point?

Your voices

Joe is a successful professional. Age thirty-three, he and his wife recently bought their first home and had their first children, twin boys.[33]

I've always resonated with the idea of self-reliance being a defining characteristic for Generation X. In fact, for as long as I can recall, I've felt fiercely independent . . . that nothing would be handed to me . . . that one has to work hard to get what they want out of life . . . that at the end of the day the only person you can trust or count on is yourself . . . that each person is responsible for their own actions. The idea of self-reliance is ingrained in my mind.

I would almost describe this Gen X attitude as a "me against the world" mentality but not in a negative or disgruntled way. It's more in the sense of: I was thrown into this complex and confusing world, and it's up to me to figure out how to live my life and succeed in what I want to accomplish in life. In other words, I am the primary author of my life, and although other people will be there to help along the way, it is ultimately up to me to choose what to write. One of my favorite quotes is Sartre's "Man is nothing else but that which he makes of himself."

With this "me versus the world" type of attitude comes a great sense of personal empowerment—that I have the power and control to determine my course in life. But on the flipside, it also comes with a healthy dose of fear and ambiguity (e.g., do I know what I want to do in life and do I know what I have to do to get there on my own?). There is almost a constant self-questioning about where I am, where I want to be, and how to get there. Sometimes that is a lonely journey that brings about fear and doubt. This in many ways relates to how one thinks about their career and what they what to do in life.

For many Gen X'ers, determining the right job or the right career is an ongoing internal battle. Who am I as a person? What am I good at? What career will allow me to accomplish my personal goals in life? In some ways, this journey is a lot about trial and error. It's about trying out jobs to see if they fit with the type of life you want to have.

I feel Gen X has viewed work as a means to end and not as an end in itself. Careers provide a means to become financially self-reliant or to feel you've worked hard and accomplished your personal goals. The problem is—once you've reached your primary goals in life, you need to make sure you are in a career that is personally fulfilling. Otherwise you'll endlessly move from job to job in an ongoing pursuit of work that is both personally rewarding and allows you to maintain previous successes (financially or otherwise). In sum, I think many of us are content with what we've accomplished thus far but are still unsatisfied in life.

In some ways I think Gen X fears that searching for that one job that would be truly fulfilling would put at risk the very things they worked so hard to achieve. Would a new career choice come with a loss of financial independence, the inability to make car or mortgage payments, things I've worked so hard to achieve? On one hand, you want to be self-reliant and have a career that resonates with your true self, but at the same time, you don't want to lose what independence you have already achieved.

How do you find a career that is both personally rewarding *and* allows you to maintain what you've already accomplished in your life? How do you take your life and your career up another level (or to put it in Maslow's terms, how do you self-actualize)? What are manageable career risks that one should take?

I think Gen X'ers are in some senses completely satisfied that they have achieved their personal ambitions, but at the same time, they are completely dissatisfied because they know ultimate self-reliance is only achieved when they are in a job that reflects their true self. I think Gen X'ers are in an ongoing pursuit to define who they are.

The Happiness of Pursuit

Joe elegantly expresses what I find at the heart of my conversations with many in Generation X: contentment with what you've accomplished thus far, but a lingering lack of satisfaction in life.

Realistically, many of you simply haven't had or spent much time thinking about life beyond "taking care of yourself." Given X'er teen and early-adult experiences, self-reliance has, until now, represented a primary and urgent life goal.

This is an important time to begin considering "What's next?" For one thing—and this may sound odd—a recession is a good time to make changes. Paul Romer, a Stanford economist, is credited with first saying what has by now become a bit of a cliché: "A crisis is a terrible thing to waste."[34] As this implies, when things are already a bit unsettled, it's often a good time to make even more significant change. For example, if your current job feels shaky, rather than rushing to find a similar position in another firm, consider if this might be the time to make a more substantial career shift. More important, feeling oriented within your life's stages—clear on where you are and thoughtful on where you'd like to head—provides its own sense of ease. There's happiness in the pursuit.

Perhaps the most creative thinker on this topic is Robert Kegan. His book, *The Evolving Self: Problem and Process in Human Development*, published in 1982, is still widely viewed as one of the most innovative and perceptive views on the intrinsic stages (rather than observable milestones) we go through as adults. Kegan suggests that *interpreting* the events in our lives—he calls it "making sense" of experience, "making meaning"—is the most basic and universal human activity.[35] In the absence of a traditional pattern of life events, the meaning making falls more heavily on your own shoulders. What's your story? And what point of the story have you reached? How do you interpret your progress and path?

For most, the early years of adulthood are spent establishing personal autonomy—your independence and self-definition. This has almost certainly been a focus of your past ten to twenty years, even stretching back into your teen years, given how quickly many of you took on responsibilities. You've been working on defining yourself, achieving in your career, and taking on roles of authority over others in the workplace and as parents.

Kegan suggests that the next step—the next intrinsic landmark along the path of adulthood—involves a shift to focus on how you connect with others.[36] It's about thinking of how your future is tied to that of others, seeing yourself as part of a network, and understanding the power of these links.

In his book *Arrested Adulthood*, James Cote worries that many people may stall before seeing themselves clearly in the context of others. For Cote, "Adulthood is about the capacity of the evolving self to make successive and successful connections to an unpredictable and changing world."[37]

As you move forward, grounding yourself within the context of others and among the intrinsic landmarks of your life will be an important step in answering the question "what's next?" In the next chapter, I'll discuss one important dimension of the context you face: the other generations in your life and the challenges each presents.

CHAPTER THREE

What Are They Thinking?

The Other Four Generations

A Boomer boss walks into a Gen X'er's office and says, "I've got great news for you! I recommended you for a promotion—and you won!"

Pause, as the Boomer waits for any obvious signs of delight from the X'er. (Boomers, for reasons I'll explain in this chapter, tend as a group to be pretty competitive; winning is a *very* big deal. So, to the Boomer, this is certain to be fantastic news.)

"Of course, it does mean you'll have to relocate. The promotion is in our Topeka office."

Pause. Dead silence from the X'er. Then, "No, thanks."

Starts off like a joke, doesn't it? But it's no joke. Here we have two generations responding to the same set of conditions in very different ways, and each generation's complete inability to comprehend why the other would react the way they do.

What happens next? The Boomer will most likely make a rapid leap to a value judgment regarding the X'er's level of gratitude for the vote of confidence and perhaps his commitment to the company and to his career. It would be a short step for the Boomer to assume that the X'er lacks ambition, confidence, or perhaps even raw intelligence. After all, how could this guy not *get* how big a deal this is?

All these judgments are wrong. But they would be the instinctive reactions of a generation that has been conditioned to look at the world only through a lens that frames events in zero-sum terms—someone wins, another loses—and in an ongoing game of musical chairs. The Boomer sees a fundamentally competitive world in which winning is the best possible outcome, no matter the cost.

Generation X sees a very different world. Most of you reading this already know what the X'er is thinking: the idea of being promoted and relocated feels not like a "win," but like being forced out along a tenuous limb that could be sawn off by a capricious corporation at any moment. Risks aside, the move would mean disrupting family and leaving friends. And there's the royally annoying fact that the Boomer just *assumed* this promotion was something to prize, without ever stopping to ask about the X'er's goals. To this X'er, the Boomer's blithe confidence in his reaction reflects the stereotypical negative traits of the Boomer generation—presumptuous, self-absorbed, and arrogant. And that, I've got to say, would be wrong too.

It's easy to form unfair and negative impressions of someone from another generation, and these impressions often lead to unintended consequences that may not be in either party's best interest.

I was teaching a class of executives recently and told this story as part of a discussion about the importance of looking at each generation's actions through their eyes, not our own. One of the participants, an X'er, shared with the group that she had just gone through an identical experience, right down to the specifics of Topeka as the targeted site for the promotion.

"What did you do?" I asked.

"I quit."

This chapter is about "them"—the other generations who share the workplace and your lives. Like you, the way they interpreted the events of their teen years—the conclusions they drew about how things work and how to succeed in life—has significant implications for the role that work plays in their lives, what they expect to receive from the work experience, how they are likely to react to specific work-related experiences, and how they relate to you.

Today, you are sharing the workplace with individuals from three other generations:

- The Traditionalists, born between 1928 and 1945
- The Boomers, born between 1946 and 1964 (or 1961)
- Generation Y, born between 1980 and 1995

And many of you have one more important generation in your lives—children in what I'm calling the Re-Generation, those born after 1995. The proportion of the workforce represented by each generation over time is shown in figure 3-1. By about 2015, Generation Y will represent the largest single segment.

FIGURE 3-1

Generational shifts in the labor force composition

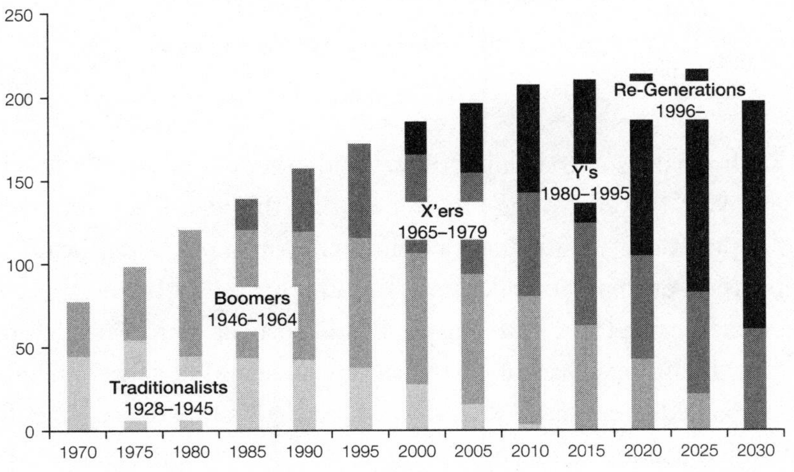

Source: U.S. Census Bureau.

Who are these other generations? Why *do* they do what they do? And *what* are they thinking?

Traditionalists

Also known as the *silent generation,* Traditionalists were born before 1946. For many of you, these are your parents. Their views substantially influenced your childhood experiences. In addition, although the number of Traditionalists present in the workplace today is decreasing, many of their assumptions are deeply embedded in the fabric of how organizations work; many corporations remain largely the product of policies and practices put in place by this generation.

Traditionalists
Born: 1928 to 1945 **Formative teen years:** The 1940s to 1950s **Age in 2009:** Sixty-four years old and older

Traditionalists in the United States and other countries that fought in World War II were young children during the war. They experienced the deprivations of wartime rationing and, in most cases, heard their Depression-era parents talk about the importance of financial security. But they became teens in the hustle-bustle postwar years. They felt patriotic pride and excitement in the boom of scientific achievement that accompanied these years. Russia launched the first manned space flight; Pan Am introduced the first around-the-world commercial air flight; Britain and France became nuclear powers; the first general-purpose electronic computer—ENIAC—was developed.

In the booming postwar economies, opportunity appeared on every street corner. Suburbs were popping up, and the dream of home ownership was suddenly in reach. Factories that had made war goods were cranking out washing machines at an astounding rate. Television purchases skyrocketed; by the end of the decade, over 80 percent of all U.S. households owned these new marvels of technology. Family dinner-table conversations probably included the amazing new conveniences just acquired by the family down the street, as "keeping up with the Joneses" became a national pastime.

Now, assume you are a teenager looking at the world for the first time at this moment. What assumptions would you form about how the world works? Whom would you respect and trust? What would you expect to do with your life? How would you measure its success?

For most who grew up in this economy of grand promise and optimism, the world was almost certainly heading in the right direction. Authority figures seemed to have things pretty well in hand. Corporate leaders and government officials warranted respect. Global issues were being resolved in reasonably satisfactory ways, and technology promised an alluring future.

This is a world that almost any teen would logically want to *join*. A teen living at this time would probably want to get a good education, leap enthusiastically into the work world, become part of the existing establishment, and attain the financial rewards that it promised—to get a piece of the pie. Financial success would serve as a measure of the extent to which you captured your share of the immediate bounty and longer-term financial security.

There were, of course, important exceptions to this sense of unlimited optimism, at least in the United States. For African Americans and other minorities, the world may have held the same allure, but not the same sense of attainability. The path to personal success in those years appeared, and often was, blocked.

Around the globe, the experiences of teens growing up in the 1940s and 1950s were vastly different.[1] For example, during these same years, India was just establishing its independence as a nation; loyalty to family and community remained critical priorities, coupled with pride in the newly forming country. In China, the end of the long Civil War resulted in the formation of the Communist-led People's Republic of China and a lengthy period of reforms under Mao Zedong. For teens, survival in this changing environment was a top priority, as the traditional way of life was, for many, abruptly altered. Clearly no one description can encompass the characteristics of the Traditionalist age cohort around the world.

In the United States and other Western nations, the Traditionalists built business organizations that reflected their values. This generation designed many of today's most successful corporations based on practices that made sense at the time; many borrowed heavily from military models—hierarchical roles; chains of command; structured career paths; banded salary levels; and well-planned, multiyear strategies. And although things may be changing, organizational structures, management practices, and policies shaped by these values are still in place in most corporations. Traditionalists tend to be respectful of authority and comfortable in hierarchy; they see value in stability and assume that fairness is provided by consistently applied rules. They are strongly influenced by financial reward and the security it can bring. While most people—in any generation—appreciate and, to one degree or another, are motivated by money, for Traditionalists, money also has a symbolic role. It serves as a metric for achievement and affirmation to themselves and others that they have attained their important teenage goals.

The assumption that money is everyone's dominant motivator and preferred reward is one of the most common sources of misunderstanding between Traditionalists (and the corporate policies they wrote) and Generation X employees. To a Traditionalist, additional monetary compensation is a big deal and a great compliment, something that should be sufficient to sway any decision. You have perhaps run into senior managers who have a very hard time understanding the trade-offs you are making and the role that money plays in choices you make.

Over the next several decades, some Traditionalists will continue to participate in the workplace. Going forward, as you work with them, keep in mind the importance they place on financial recognition, security, and hierarchy. Individuals in this generation are unlikely to be effective and engaged participants in the workforce unless these assumptions about how things are "supposed" to work are acknowledged and, to the extent possible, accommodated.

Boomers

The Boomer generation's teen years were the 1960s and 1970s, an unsettling period that yielded a generation with dramatically different perspectives than their parents had of the type of relationships they would form with corporations, peers, and family, about the importance and definition of financial success, and about the ultimate objectives for their lives.

Boomers
Born: 1946 to 1964 (or 1961) **Formative teen years:** 1960s and 1970s **Age in 2009:** Forty-five (or forty-eight) to sixty-three years old

Boomers' teen years were ones filled with causes and revolution. The 1960s and 1970s were decades of general unrest and discontent in many parts of the world. In the United States, teenage Boomers saw the assassinations of idealistic leaders—John Kennedy, Robert Kennedy, Malcolm X, and Martin Luther King Jr. They experienced the Vietnam War, widespread protests, the civil rights movement, and, toward the end of this period, Watergate and Richard Nixon's resignation.

The sense of unrest was pervasive in many parts of the world. Nearly three hundred thousand boat people fled Vietnam; the Cultural Revolution was underway in the People's Republic of China; there was rioting in France, Germany, and Italy and a revolution in Czechoslovakia.

Not surprisingly, growing up amid these events caused many Boomers, regardless of political persuasion, to conclude that the world was not working all that well—that it needed to be changed. Even worse, to many Boomers, the adults in charge didn't appear to be making the right decisions, setting the right course, or necessarily even telling the truth. Many Boomers developed skeptical, even cynical, attitudes toward authority. Their world was one in which authority figures were suspect. Many concluded that they needed to get personally involved. Their logical desire was not to *join* a world that was by and large headed in the right direction, as the Traditionalists did—but to *change* a world that had clearly gone off course.

Many Boomers did not see eye to eye with their parents. In fact, in a survey conducted in 1974, 40 percent of Boomer teens said that they'd be better off with *no* parents.[2] Most Boomers couldn't wait to escape from their parents' control, moving off to distant locations and creating independent lives as soon as possible.

And the numbers! Boomers grew up in a world that was, in many ways, "too small" for their cohort. Many went to school in temporary buildings because the schools hadn't yet expanded to accommodate the increased number of students. There were too few sports teams for all to play, too few places in colleges. As a result, competition runs deeply through Boomer assumptions about how the world works. Their conceptual model is one of a zero-sum, win-lose game. Today, most still *love* to win. I sometimes think you could put a bow around just about anything, give it to a Boomer as a prize, and she'd be pleased.

Most Boomers jumped into the workforce with passion and commitment. They played by the rules they found there and competed their way up the corporate ladders. They may not have liked them much, but they quickly fell in line. They tend to like merit-based systems and use both money and position to measure the degree to which they are winning. As a generation, Boomers tend to value *individual* achievement and *individual* recognition. They have played with abandon and only recently have begun to pause long enough to inquire about the true value of the prize.

So, for both Boomers and Traditionalists, money does work as a primary reward and motivation. Both are likely to assume that if they offer you enough money, you will happily take on whatever role is presented. But it also plays a different role for these two generations. As I've noted, Traditionalists see money as a symbol that they have successfully joined the business "club" and are reaping the benefits of membership. It also connotes security. But for Boomers, money tends to be a symbol of competitive success—of winning.

This competitive streak has served almost like a manual override for many Boomers' original teenage intentions and works against the characteristics that might have allied Boomers and X'ers—Boomers' anti-authoritarian views and X'ers' skepticism.

Your voices

Most X'ers are aware, if only subliminally, that the rise of the original Yuppies in the early eighties coincided with the exact point at which the Boomers decided to throw in the towel on saving the world and began, instead, doing lucrative consulting work for Union Carbide. "Much of the energy and optimism and passion of the '60s seems to have been turned inward, to lives, careers, apartments and dinners," *Newsweek* noted in its "Year of the Yuppie" cover story at the end of 1984.[3]

Boomers' schizophrenic mix of idealism and competitive success quite understandably drew the skepticism and scorn of young X'ers. Teen years full of idealism and defiance were followed by a frantic climb up the corporate ladder and conformation to the very establishment they had rallied against as teens. To many X'ers, all this came across as pretentious self-glorification and, at times, a delusional reflection of a life Boomers chose not to lead. To many X'ers, Boomers are masters of denying reality and ignoring the unpleasant truths.

On the other hand, to Boomers, X'ers often seem completely indecipherable. Competition—a cardinal element of the Boomer psyche—appears not to motivate X'ers. Your willingness to quit and go elsewhere and your (outspoken) irreverence can strike Boomers as almost shockingly inappropriate. Your expectation to be treated individually—to be allowed to play the game by your own rules—contrasts with Boomers' willingness to play by established rules in competition for individual rewards. To Boomers, you can seem disconnected, cynical, disloyal, and unwilling to accept challenge and responsibility. As one Boomer said in response to a post, "I find Gen X'ers perplexing and difficult to manage because I do not understand them."

Your voices

In my last office, I was a Gen X'er working with a large number of Baby Boomers. There is a definite culture difference between the two groups despite an often small separation in age. Gen X'ers are more concerned with finding the right job for them, regardless of which company, instead of sticking with a company and hoping to climb the ladder. I have found many Boomers to be very ambitious and concerned with climbing the ladder. Many are unhappy in their jobs, yet don't consider leaving their organizations. Gen X'ers, on the other hand, are often more concerned with a work-life balance where they "work to live" instead of "live to work." Free time is highly valued, probably more so than money for many. We have seen Boomers fill and stay in management/leadership positions, thus resigning us to remain in the rank and file. We tend to job-hop more than Boomers, since

company loyalty is not something we expect, having seen and been affected by the downsizing of the eighties and nineties. Boomers are seen by Gen X'ers as a "me" generation; it's all about them. They got the jobs and the houses, and we were left with the leftovers.

Today, many Boomers retain a strong desire to make a difference. Increasingly, many are confronting the reality that they have not followed through on their teenage intentions. As they turn fifty or sixty, many are looking to refocus their lives, redirecting their energy and attention to "doing more." Going forward, look for ways to tap Boomers' experience and reemerging idealism (as Barack Obama appears to have done in the selection of his top team) to help achieve the goals you set.

Generation Y

Over the past decade, Generation Y, also often called the *Millennial Generation,* has joined the workforce. Born between 1980 and 1995, the Y's are the largest consumer group and soon will be the largest employee group in the history of the United States, more than 70 million strong. They represent an even larger proportion of the population globally. The large size of this generational cohort means that they will have a significant influence on the world in which we live and work. They have been teens since the mid-1990s.

Generation Y

Born: 1980 to 1995

Teen years: Mid-1990s and 2000s

Age in 2009: Fourteen to twenty-nine years old

Y's grew up in the midst of a world struggling to comprehend the escalating terrorism and school violence dominating the headlines. Beginning with the Lockerbie air disaster, in which Pan Am Flight 103 was destroyed by a bomb, that occurred before Y's were teens (in 1988), through the bombings at the World Trade Center, Oklahoma City, and the Atlanta Olympics during the 1990s; the bombings of the Madrid and London subways in 2004 and 2005, respectively; and, of course, the events of September 11, 2001, this generation has been engulfed in a world colored by inexplicable and unpredictable events. And the violent incidents in schools during Y's own school years—Columbine and Virginia Tech in the United States, Beslan in Russia, and, sadly, many more—had an even more significant impact, being aimed straight at their age cohort.

Terrorism differs from war in one important way. Everyone who goes to war recognizes at some level that bad things could happen. No one goes to school expecting that bad things could happen. Acts of terrorism are fundamentally *random*. Growing up when they did has left Y's with a conceptual model that is heavily based on unpredictability (have you noticed how frequently the word *random* peppers their speech?). For many, living life to the fullest—now—has become an important and understandable priority. A sense of impatience—I prefer the word *immediacy*—will be *the* single most salient characteristic defining this generation throughout their lives and not something they will "outgrow."

In contrast to the external world, and perhaps in part because of it, Y's have been blessed with an almost cocoon level of parental attention—immersed in a very pro-child culture—in contrast with the latchkey childhood of many X'ers. This is a generation that grew up eating off red plates with "You Are Special Today" on the rim; one that was continually reminded that they could do anything they set their minds to. Movies in which kids were horrible or scary began to fail at the box office during their youth, replaced by *Three Men and a Baby* and *Parenthood*. Boomers soaked up the humanistic theories of childhood psychology and became increasingly involved in their children's lives.

Today, Y's and their parents share many common interests, from movies and music to recreational activities and charitable concerns. The result is a generation of young adults who like and trust not only their parents, but most of the older adults in their lives. "Their connection to their parents is deep and strong," says Middlebury College psychology professor Barbara Hofer. "They say, 'My parents are my best friends.' People would have seen that as aberrant a generation ago, as pathological."[4]

Their behavior in the workplace can strike many of you as inappropriate. Fearless and blunt, they offer their opinions freely, without regard for corporate hierarchy and with no sense of what would be considered "proper" business protocol, and seem to expect everyone to be interested in their point of view. The strong bonds they've formed with their families are easy to misinterpret as dependence and can seem very odd to many of you who made your decisions independently or based on advice from friends.

Your voices

"Yes, there's a revolution under way among today's kids—*a good news revolution,*" demographers Neil Howe and William Strauss would write in 2000 in *Millennials Rising: The Next Great Generation,* barely containing their glee . . . These are not my italics, by the way. They're in the book. Howe and Strauss must have been really excited about this . . . they go on to rave about how these super-duper millennials are optimists! Who accept authority! And follow rules! *Oh, happy happy, joy joy.*[5]

Other aspects of Generation Y's childhood experiences were very different from yours and left them with a very different perspective on money, working mothers, and, no surprise, technology.

Unlike your experience of watching parents and other adults go through the downsizings and layoffs of the 1980s, Generation Y has experienced, until very recently, an unprecedented bull market and economic prosperity. Despite current economic difficulties, Y's tend to have a rosy outlook on the long-term opportunities ahead. This sense of optimism, along with the safety net that their warm relationships with their parents provides, is prompting Y's to approach work in a way that, again, can be highly annoying to X'ers, almost as if they hope to be paid "volunteers." Many Y's are shopping around, in what David Brooks has called their period of "odyssey years," for organizations that they *really* want to join.[6]

Where Generation X's experience of women working outside the home was one of change and upheaval—mom going off to work—for Generation Y, mom has always been at work. Generation Y's attitudes on this issue are both more relaxed and also more *choice*-oriented than any generation before.[7] They are accustomed to seeing women in leadership roles and know that women *can,* if they choose, work full time and rear children. In many cases, their own mothers did it.

Generation Y is the first generation of unconsciously competent users of digital technology. Generation X grew up alongside the Internet. You learned to use the technology as its influence spread and as you or your contemporaries developed new applications. Generation Y woke up and the Internet was *there,* always on. They have never known a world that wasn't wired. Technology is ubiquitous and an essential part of how they operate day to day. Y's are not stressed by it and can be dismissive of those who struggle with it. Y's reach out openly to peers for vetted sources of information and share it with wide groups of friends and acquaintances. Unlike your tighter "tribes," Y's typically operate with broader and looser networks.

Your voices

They did everything in groups, they even dated in groups. They moved in noisy little packs . . . they networked, they sought out mentors, they kept each other in line. They wanted to connect with everyone; they wanted the world to cuddle up with them on Friendster and Facebook. They were unfamiliar with the notion of privacy. Solitude made them . . . uncomfortable.[8]

Relationships between X'ers and Y's in the workplace are mixed. Many Y's do report having strong relationships with X'er colleagues. As one said, "They can remember what it was like to start out as a professional and are more likely to offer unsolicited advice or to assist me with a problem. My higher-up supervisors tend to be too busy for such a relationship, and I tend to be more formal with them."

But many do not. As another said, "The Y finds the X'er not competent to be his boss, feels that the X'er is diffusing his enthusiasm by not appreciating his work and ideas, and thinks the X'er underestimates his capacity. These reasons may be right or wrong; but . . . it is high time for the X'er to realize that Y is to be treated with more respect and consideration."

The Re-Generation

I suspect that the next major generation began to take shape in 2008. Individuals who were eleven to thirteen in 2008 experienced an environment that was substantively different than that of the past fifteen years. I propose we call this new generation the Re-Generation, or Re-Gens, for reasons I'll explain next.

The Re-Generation (or "Re-Gens")
Born: 1995–1997 onward **Teen years:** 2008 onward **Age in 2009:** Fourteen and younger

The year 2008 *felt* different. Collective optimism was doused with the cold-water realization that globally we are facing significant, seemingly intractable problems on multiple fronts. The inconvenient truths of the past half-century settled around our shoulders, and preteens were not unaware of these issues or their complexity. The mental map for eleven- to thirteen-year-olds began forming based on a world with finite limits and no easy answers.

- They have not missed the messages regarding layoffs and challenges to global banks and corporations.
- Most are very aware that the polar ice caps are melting and the march of the penguins is slowing to a halt.
- They know why many families are vacationing in the backyard and understand that high gas prices are related to diminishing global supply of energy.
- Many understand that other resources are limited, as well. Their geography lessons have given them a sense of the vital role water plays in politics and our future.
- Whatever they or their parents think about the war in Iraq and the Middle East in general, it's likely that they have absorbed the complexity of the situation. I doubt they've heard anyone offering simple, quick solutions.
- It would have been almost impossible for them to escape the phrase *housing crisis* or even *recession*, although most are probably too young to understand how such disasters came to be.

This new generation has been swaddled in reality. They've been weaned on reality TV—not the "we can do it" optimism of the Boomer's *Mickey Mouse Club*, the upbeat interpretation of shifting family structures of the X'ers' *Facts of Life*, or the Y's glamorous escape into the unreality of *90210*, but the images of real people taking on big challenges, typically in pursuit of the *new* Great American Goal: $1 million.

Unlike Gen Y's, members of the Re-Generation do not remember 9/11. The youngest Y's would have been seven that day, probably the dividing line for those who might remember. For them, it will be a history lesson taught in school.

Many Re-Gens will, of course, remember the astonishing political events of 2008—the United States's election of its first African American president. They all will grow up with the sense of personal possibility that event conveys. The young people who looked up from childhood in 2008 to form their first views of how the world works are being imprinted with images of a different world than you or I saw when we formed our first mental models.

This will be a generation of realists, of pragmatists. Truth, finite limits, conservation, trade-offs, balance—these I suspect will be themes of our newest generation. I suggest the Re-Generation has a number of appropriate associations:

- Reality. This generation is coming of age in a world that is grappling with some difficult, inconvenient truths. They will form a mental map based on a world with limits and no easy answers.
- Realists. Theirs will be a generation of pragmatists, raised by their down-to-earth Gen X parents to consider trade-offs and long-term balance.
- Restraint and responsibility. Necessary postures in today's world.
- Renewable energy, recycling, reducing carbon emissions, and resource limitations. Challenges they will face.
- Resentment. That older adults have been poor stewards of our world.
- Recession. Economic conditions over the next decade will be more conservative than the upbeat decades past.

To rethink, renew, and regenerate are the challenges this generation will face.

For many of you, these are your children. Their priorities will influence your decisions about where you focus your efforts over the next decades. Your concerns about making organizations more adaptive to their needs will shape many of your goals.

Across the Ages

The primary value of generational analysis is to make the actions of others a little more understandable. By understanding other generations' perspectives, we are better able to position our ideas and requests in ways that are likely to have positive results and avoid at least some of the frustrations of today's workplace.

Perhaps my most important suggestion is simply to remember that the way something looks to you is probably not the way it looks to others. Looking at the situation through others' lenses will give you a clue about why they do what they do. As you work with people from other generations and other backgrounds, think about their formative years for clues about why they may see things differently than you do.

Working with people of all ages is critically important to your success in today's multigenerational workplace. Understanding why colleagues from other generations behave the way they do will give you an advantage as you work with them—whether they be your bosses, colleagues, clients, partners, or customers. Understanding their priorities, including those of the Re-Generation, will help shape yours.

Part II

Evaluate Your Next Steps

CHAPTER FOUR

What Do *You* Want?

Resetting Your Life and Work Priorities

Throughout my research, several closely intertwined themes stand out as nearly universal desires for most members of Generation X. As a generation, you tend to value:

- The ability to handle whatever comes your way—to be self-reliant
- Money—particularly to the extent it contributes to your sense of security and self-reliance
- Being good parents—for those of you who have chosen to go that route
- Good friends—often representing bonds as strong as or stronger than family
- The ability to choose how you spend your time—which for many of you translates into the ability to balance work and nonwork-related priorities

Beyond these universal themes, as individuals, you all have strong personal preferences for the characteristics of work that you find most rewarding and engaging. Later in this chapter, I'll share frameworks for thinking about what you enjoy most. But first, let's look at some common threads.

Shared Desires of Your Generation

Many of your generation's nearly universal goals are extensions of the life experiences you've had thus far.

Control over "If" Through Security and Self-Reliance

As teens, many of you experienced seemingly rock-solid components of life shifting in unpredictable ways. From an early age, you have been intensely aware of your position in a precarious world. And so it's no surprise that many X'ers' most fundamental desire is to be able to handle the unexpected "ifs" in life. For most of you, "Would I be prepared *if* something bad were to happen?" is the question that lingers in your thoughts about the future.

Your voices

Gen X's self-reliance is not the same bootstrapping mentality of the Depression generation. It lacks that *Holy cow, I'd better do this myself or else!* urgency but [rather] is born from a feeling of almost existential helplessness.[1]

While Boomers and Traditionalists are interested in *job* security, X'ers want *career* or life security, which you seek in multiple ways. For some of you, it translates into a desire for control over your own destiny, pushing you in entrepreneurial directions. For many others, it heightens your desire to maintain a broad base of marketable skills and a willingness to continue evolving into new skill sets as job availability shifts. For most, it means having multiple options always in mind, *if* something bad were to block one route.

Your voices

We watched as major companies threw responsibility out the window when it came to their employees and laid them off right before they were due to retire, thus avoiding having to pay pensions. We were promised good jobs if we went to college, but when we graduated, no good jobs were to be found. We lost the concept of loyalty to a corporation. We became free agents, changing jobs that didn't suit our lifestyles, retraining when necessary for completely different careers than we'd first been educated for. We were called slackers and cynical, yet we became independent and entrepreneurial out of necessity.[2]

Options assuage concerns about being backed into a dead-end corner. And a perceived lack of options is making many members of Generation X feel increasingly uneasy within corporations. As you ascend in the hierarchy, for most, the career paths narrow. You become increasingly specialized in one area and, as a result, feel more vulnerable to downturns in that niche. My research shows that you are more likely than any other generational cohort to *fear* being laid off, perhaps justifiably.[3] Anecdotal evidence from the early stages of the recession that began in 2008 indicates that your generation may be the hardest hit.

Few of you have reached a high enough point in the corporate hierarchy to feel that you have control over the big decisions. This growing sense of unease is causing many of you to consider leaving corporate life and to move on to other alternatives that feel as if they provide a greater sense of self-reliance, control over your own destiny, and, therefore, security.

Your voices

I have to say I don't feel I am being given any other choice but to make alternative plans. Why should I be loyal and trust an organization . . .? I see no reason whatever to trust them, nor do I. I am making plans to take care of myself by creating options that will allow me to secure the longevity of my career so I can care for my family as best I can through the remainder of my work career and into retirement.

Importantly, it is the desire for options and greater control over your own destiny that is prompting many of you to consider leaving corporate life, not, in most cases, some type of *a priori* quest for independence. For you, there is no manifest destiny in the creation of a "free agent nation," as is often implied in the writings about your generation. In a study of Generation X professionals in the United States and Canada, 47 percent said they would be happy spending the rest of their careers with their current organization, 85 percent cared a great deal about the future of their organization, and 83 percent said they were willing to go beyond what is normally expected in order to ensure the success of that organization.[4] Another study concluded that Gen X employees were no more likely than their age counterparts in 1977 to plan to leave their current employers within the next year (43 percent somewhat or very likely).[5] Yet another study concluded that Gen X'ers are Traditionalists at heart: respondents placed high value on company loyalty and work-life balance; nearly half would be content to spend the rest of their careers with their current companies.[6]

But despite these leanings, the reality of your careers is that most of you have not found organizations in which you feel comfortable staying for long periods of time. Your desire for self-reliance wins out. Most corporations are unable to address the *if* that overrides your thoughts.

Money

Perhaps one of the biggest misconceptions about Generation X is that you are less interested in material wealth than were previous generations.

Being responsible for money may lack novelty for some of you, but that doesn't mean it is not important. Your generation has been participating in discretionary spending since you were teenagers, and most of you would like to create or maintain a pretty ambitious level of affluence. Over ten years ago, *Time*'s "New American Dream" study concluded that the majority of X'ers believe that material possessions are, in fact, very important.[7]

Perhaps some of you did start your adult life with little interest in money, but by the mid-1990s that changed for even the most hardy holdouts from the commercial world.

Your voices

One day everyone woke up and discovered money. A memo went out.[8]

The dot-com boom launched for many on the day of Netscape's initial public offering (IPO) in August 1995, when one of your own, Marc Andreessen, age twenty-four, was suddenly worth $58 million. For five years, until the stock market crash in 2000, your generation was front and center in the Internet excitement and the promise it held of sudden and extraordinary riches.

Money is especially important now, not only because of the growing demands on your resources, as discussed in chapter 2, but also because it provides greater protection against the *ifs*. With money, you have more options.

To Be Good Parents

X'ers are dedicated to being good parents. This may seem like an obvious statement, but it represents a subtle change from the way Boomers have viewed child rearing. Boomers want their *children* to be successful. You want to be successful as *parents*.

Boomers have gone to extraordinary lengths to secure their children's success in life, from investments in their earliest education to kamikaze-like strikes into any institution that threatens to thwart junior's progress. They spend a lot of time with their children and have developed warm, friendlike relationships.

X'ers unquestionably share the same desire to help their children succeed, but an important part of the focus is on being a successful parent, with all that that entails: time, attention, structure, and protection. It is parenting as many believe it *should* be done.

Many of you want a different relationship with your kids than the one you had with your parents. You feel strongly about providing a different childhood experience. Others of you, particularly those who grew up with Traditionalist parents, are looking to recreate a degree of the structure and security you experienced during your childhood, rather than what you perceive as the freewheeling Boomer parenting style.

Your voices

A thirty-four-year-old Gen X mother with two daughters, six and eleven, who says she will never do what her own Boomer mom did—work full time.

A lot of times my mom had to work late. I was a latchkey child. I came home to a house alone. I cannot even imagine doing that with my children.[9]

The rub is that this desire conflicts with the work patterns many of you have established. Gen X women with children are much more likely to be working outside the home than women in earlier generations. In fact, the involvement of working mothers represents one of the most significant changes in your generation's workforce participation. Women with children under the age of three are almost twice as likely to be working as Boomer women with children of that age were: 63 versus 33

FIGURE 4-1

Labor force participation rate for women age 25 to 34 with children

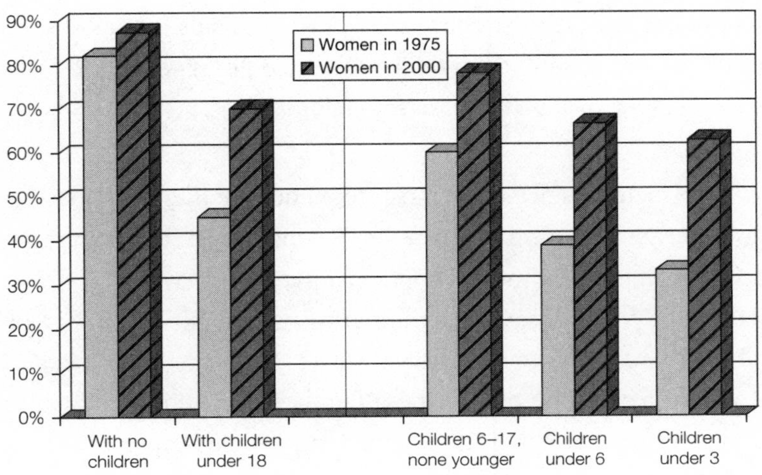

Source: Marisa DiNatale and Stephanie Boraas, "The Labor Force Experience of Women from 'Generation X'," *Monthly Labor Review*, Bureau of Labor Statistics, 2002.

percent. There has also been a significant change among women with older children, those between the ages of six and seventeen. Only 60 percent of Boomer women in this category participated in the workforce, while almost 80 percent of X'er women do (see figure 4-1).[10]

Although you are working long and hard, the priority you place on parenting may shape some of your views toward workplace success. Many of you say that you are less interested in climbing to the top of the corporate ladder if it means giving up family time.[11]

The desire to be a good parent is very evident among both Gen X women and men. Despite the difficulty of balancing work and family time, Gen X dads are spending a lot of time with their children. Fathers in 2002 spent 2.7 hours each workday caring for children, almost an hour more than fathers in 1977 and a 50 percent increase in male parenting time. During the same twenty-five-year period, working mothers' hours spent caring for children stayed roughly the same, about 3.3 hours a day.[12]

Your voices

Parental pressures [are] at their peak. I can't tell you how many times my boss has said: "Say goodbye to the wife and kids for the next two weeks." My response: "I don't think so!" I am determined not to be like my own father. I *will* be there for my children.

For some members of Gen X, most frequently mothers, commitment to parenting means choosing to stay at home when your children are young. Some X'er women view motherhood as a permanent workforce exit, but many more of you are viewing childrearing as a career break, just one of several roles you will enjoy during your lives. You are stepping in and out of the workforce, taking time to raise families, worrying less than in the past about getting permanently sidelined in your career plans.

Your voices

I am thirty-nine years old. I left the corporate world four years ago to raise my children. I tried to work part time. My manager supported it, but that's where the support ended. I still feel that I have a valuable contribution to make. And I would welcome the opportunity to work part time in a capacity similar to what I left. If corporations want loyal, committed employees in their thirties and forties, they should look at stay-at-home moms. Let us make our contributions. Just know we won't sacrifice the raising of our children.

As a generation, you are working hard to prioritize family and protect the quality of family life. Some observers expect that as you move into your peak family-raising years, we will see an increase in the traditional "married couple with children" family structure.[13] In some cases, among more affluent Gen X moms, not working outside the home is even becoming the new status symbol.[14]

The desire to be a good parent is one of the major influences on another common thread: the desire for control over your time in order to balance work with other priorities.

Balance

One of the terms Douglas Coupland coined to describe Generation X was "lessness." He defined it as a philosophy whereby one reconciles oneself with diminishing expectations of material wealth: "I've given up wanting to make a killing or be a big shot. I just want to find happiness and maybe open up a little roadside cafe in Idaho."[15]

Your voices

Some of the signpost Gen X movies . . . seem to revel in the perversely liberating thrill of being marginalized. X'ers shine when expectations are lowered: one of those high-paid Boomer career coaches might come to the conclusion that we just, you know, *define success differently*. We expect to be obsolete.[16]

None of you I've interviewed have spoken of an expectation of obsolescence, but I do find that previous generations' definitions of success are not ones that you buy into. While money is important, many of you believe that happiness in life cannot be achieved without a healthy commitment to outside interests, including a rich family and social life.[17] You value balance and flexibility broadly, not only to meet parenting demands, but to meet your vision of the life you'd like to lead. And you value the satisfaction of work well done.

Your views are a significant contrast to Boomers', many of whom, as I discussed in chapter 3, have been deeply committed to winning and willing to make significant sacrifices to achieve victory. It's also subtly different from Y's who are intent on optimizing each day's experience.

Your voices

I'm thirty-three. I have a great educational pedigree, good experience, and don't really care that much about my title as long as I'm being paid well. However, I simply don't see the point of putting in fifty-hour-plus workweeks. Career is great, but it's important to have time for your family and yourself. If the corporation I work for doesn't like that attitude, tough luck.

When I was thirty-three and single, I was working nights and weekends to build a career. It took a husband and two preschoolers to make me realize, at forty, that I had to find a better balance of work and personal satisfaction. I did it by reducing my work hours, taking a salary cut, and dialing back my ambitions.[18]

Both X'er men and women are reassessing their roles in the workplace and in the home. Gen X women are looking for a sense of balance and feel entitled to be both good workers and good mothers.

Discontent among men trying to balance work and family demands has risen within your generation. Gen X women experienced about the same amount of conflict in meeting work and family demands in 2002 as your Boomer counterparts did in 1977, but men's sense of frustration rose sharply. In 1977, about one-third of men reported tension around the juggling act; in 2002, more than half of you did.[19] A growing number of Gen X men have intentionally slowed down their careers. Many of you are looking at what you may have missed when you were growing up and have decided to create a different experience for yourself and your family.

Your voices

I and 99 percent of my friends and coworkers who are X'ers are frantically trying to create the perfect balance of professional versus personal. Most important to us are our continuous attempts at bolstering our relationships with family members.

Not only the demands of family prompt X'ers' decisions to scale back; sometimes the trade-offs in the effort of "making it" are too steep. Gen X women, watching the Boomers' attempts to break the glass ceiling at work, have not been overly impressed. Many of you think that Boomer women paid too high a price and were forced to focus solely on work in order to succeed. In your eyes, Boomers may have blazed a trail, but the promise of "having it all" was one that they could not achieve. You tend to be more realistic. Many women in their twenties and thirties want to have more control over their lives, even if it means forgoing the top positions.

Your voices

We're not seeing a lot of great stories of "having it all," so what happens to those of us who bought that line and now find ourselves with less than half: family but no work, or all work but no family? The system hasn't changed; men are still at the top, with a few token women who make everyone feel great. Let's not even bother trying to get to the top.[20]

The "not having it all" phenomenon is borne out by the statistics. Only 67 percent of top executive women with MBAs are married, compared with 84 percent of men with the same work success. Nearly 75 percent of the men have children, while only 49 percent of the women do.[21] It's easy to conclude that top executive women couldn't have gotten to where they are today if they'd tried to do it all.

Your voices

When in college, I was ingrained with all these options, all these possibilities still waiting around the corner. Having played the corporate game for a while, I noticed that those options might be there, but

mainly for men willing to use their elbows . . . I've already left the corporate game, and if all goes well, I will [soon] return to . . . the small company that I helped build, that I feel passionate about. And you know what? I will do that in forty hours a week (instead of sixty), earn substantially less but have time for a private life, creative projects, and friends. I am thirty-three now and just realizing what matters most. Playing the corporate game is not it.

Today, whatever the cause, 37 percent of professional women are leaving the workforce. Those who leave stay out an average of 2.2 years, then 93 percent try to opt back in. While 74 percent do find work, only 40 percent find work they call satisfying.[22]

And you are deeply committed to creating a good life. Your life outside the workplace, whether or not that includes children, is important enough to warrant rethinking your commitment to the organization. In one study of your generation, over 70 percent of respondents rated companionship, a loving family, and enjoying life as extremely important. By contrast, less than 20 percent said earning a lot of money and becoming an influential leader were extremely important goals.[23]

For many in Generation X, your physical home plays an important role in setting the stage for the experience you want to create for yourself, your spouse, and your children. You generally value a comfortable home that reflects your tastes and styles. As one writer said, "Gen X women—married or not, mothers or not—seem bent on creating a new, more mature, quintessence of adulthood, of career, of home. Equal parts traditionalism, irony, and iconoclasm, thirtysomethings' universe—including work and leisure—gravitates around the home."[24]

Your voices

Gen X, whether they're single women or single men or couples, want a home. They want it to feel like a home. They want "the Martha Effect."[25]

Finding Your Individual Desires and Priorities

These general X'er priorities are the context for considering your personal preferences for work through the frameworks that follow. I have a very simple point of view: organizations are all different, people are all different, and the key to success (both yours and the organization's) is to find a match.

Thinking about selecting your type and place of work based on finding the best match with your specific preferences is a good strategy for everyone, but particularly so for members of Generation X. It fits your philosophy: you wouldn't anticipate that anything would be right for everyone. You expect alternatives. And you value finding your own unique path.

Finding what is engaging for you should be a very personal quest. Priorities for what you want back from the work experience vary. Although the goals I discussed earlier are widely shared among your generation, the emphasis among them and the degree to which you want to achieve them through your work experience depend on your individual preferences. Some of you care deeply about social connections and friendships you can form in the workplace. Others care about the opportunity for creative expression. Still others want to make as much money as possible in a way that is as flexible and low commitment as possible. Some people have high tolerance for risk and love the rush of a high-risk, high-reward environment. Others crave the steady dependability of a well-structured, long-term climb up the career ladder. Some of you want to give back to others or make a lasting difference in the world.

Individuals also like to work in very different ways. Some prefer open-ended challenges; others, highly structured tasks. Some like to be part of a team; others prefer to work alone. Some need and enjoy a great deal of day-to-day guidance; others work best with hands-off managers who leave them to figure out the best approach.

My research shows that organizations with highly engaged employees tend to be idiosyncratic—they have very distinctive and, in some instances, "weird" practices—and have attracted people who are passionate about the unique features of the work environment offered. People who love their work are those who love the specific characteristics of the organization and tasks they've chosen.

Achieving a comfortable fit with work is worth going the extra mile. Having a goal of enjoying work just makes sense. We all spend a lot of time there and, based on your long life expectancies, Generation X will undoubtedly spend a lot more. Despite the difficulty involved, don't give up on the ideal of finding work that you enjoy as much as possible.

Many people find themselves at times caught up in doing something because they think it's going to lead to something else, even though they don't enjoy it or think it's worthwhile. And many career counselors' advice seems to point in this direction: grit your teeth and do things that will position you for success. Unfortunately, instrumental reasons usually don't work out. Events are too complicated and unpredictable.

The most successful people make decisions because they think the immediate choice is inherently valuable, regardless of where it may or may not lead. They take a job or join a company because it will let them do interesting work in a place they love, even if they don't know exactly where it will lead. They understand what most career guides don't: career satisfaction comes from following your heart.[26]

Corporate leaders are also coming to understand the importance of attracting and retaining employees who genuinely enjoy both the work and the characteristics and values of the organization: employees who are more likely to be engaged. From a hard-nosed, bottom-line perspective, companies suffer financially when engagement is lacking and are often plagued by high turnover, poorly treated customers, and a lack of innovative ideas.[27] Organizations where people love their work realize major returns on those efforts: higher levels of productivity and profitability, increased organizational stability, and greater innovation. This level of success undoubtedly comes from the high levels of discretionary effort that these employees *choose* to invest in the job—more energy and initiative than would be needed only to get by.[28] Bodies and hands just aren't enough; hearts and minds are essential.

It's a win/win—for you and for the organization you join—to take the time to find work and a workplace you love.

Middlescence

Unfortunately, many in your generation today are not there yet. Many are burned out, bottlenecked, and bored. In research that my colleagues and I have done on employee experiences, we have heard many stories of midcareer malaise, a phenomenon we call *middlescence*. Take the case of one productive and well-respected middle manager in his forties. He was sandwiched between obligations at work and home, and his work group was demoralized after two rounds of downsizing. The company's structure had flattened, leaving fewer possibilities for promotion. Despite his respect for the company and fundamental enjoyment of his work, he was burned out. "This isn't how my life and career were supposed to play out," he told the employee counselor. "I don't know how much longer I can cope."[29] This is a pretty typical expression of the middlescence dilemma.

Your voices

People often burn out around ten to fifteen years into a career. It is just that now it is more acceptable to be vocal and honest about this.

Midcareer employees (those between the ages of thirty-five and fifty-four) work longer hours than their older and younger counterparts, with 30 percent saying they work fifty or more hours per week. Yet only 43 percent are passionate about their jobs, only 33 percent feel energized by their work, 36 percent say they feel that they are in dead-end jobs, and more than 40 percent report feelings of burnout. They are the most likely to feel at a dead end in their corporate careers. Midcareer employees are the least likely to say that their workplace is congenial and fun or that it offers ample opportunity to try new things.[30] The largest decline in job satisfaction over the past ten years occurred among workers between the ages of thirty-five and forty-four.[31]

In short, far too many of you are working more, enjoying it less, worrying about the next step, and looking for meaningful alternatives.

Getting Engaged with Work

How do you feel about your current job?

- I love it and want to know how to be more successful, in the ways I personally define "success."
- I used to love it, but it's gotten far less enjoyable in the past years; perhaps I'm in middlescence.
- I've never really connected with this work or this organization; it may be a "good" job, but it doesn't excite me personally.

In later chapters, I discuss approaches for being more successful and for renewing your enjoyment of work if you're feeling burned out. But it's hardly worth working to be more successful at something you fundamentally don't enjoy. The foundation needs to be right for you.

Consider how you feel with your current work by taking the quiz in worksheet 4-1.

WORKSHEET 4-1

Quiz: *Are you engaged?*

1. Are you excited and enthusiastic about your job? [Y] [N]
2. Do you ever lose yourself—forget about time and place—because you're so wrapped up in the work you truly enjoy? [Y] [N]
3. Do you happily focus on your work, versus waiting eagerly for that next email or IM to arrive and break the boredom? [Y] [N]
4. Do you voluntarily invest extra effort or produce significantly more than your work requires? [Y] [N]
5. Is what you're doing so inherently interesting that you think about it "after hours," for example, in the car or on the way home? [Y] [N]
6. Do you routinely search for ways to improve things at work or volunteer for more difficult assignments? [Y] [N]
7. Is your enthusiasm contagious—does your passion for work encourage others to join in? [Y] [N]
8. Are you proud to identify with your work? [Y] [N]

If you answered no to more than three of these questions, you're not enjoying your work nearly enough. It's time to consider moving to work that you will find more meaningful.

My overarching advice is to find a *type* of work and a *place* of work that suits you. The good news is that organizations differ substantially in terms of culture, values, and approaches. Potential colleagues have very different philosophies and values. And various types of work bring characteristically different rewards, risks, and rhythms. If you don't like where you are now or what you're doing, chances are there's a much better match out there somewhere.

Later in this chapter, I'll provide some practical worksheets for distilling what it is you love. I'll help you think about the characteristics of work that you will personally enjoy. But first, consider two analogies for engagement that you have probably already experienced in other parts of your life. As you read, identify activities that create "flow" for you. What gives you energy rather than drains it?[32]

Remember, engagement is not the same as satisfaction. Satisfaction with work focuses on what makes you "not unhappy": adequate benefits, safe and nondiscriminatory work environment, reasonable pay, and so on. Engagement is about being deeply committed to and energized by your work.

Flow

Have you ever been so deeply into something such as an athletic activity or playing a musical instrument that the moment stands out as one of the best in your life? That the activity feels almost effortless?

Try to remember a time in your life when you've felt:

- Completely involved, focused, and concentrating
- A sense of ecstasy, of being outside everyday reality
- Great inner clarity, knowing what needs to be done and how well it is going

- Confident that your skills are adequate to the task and neither anxious nor bored
- Serene, with no worries
- Thoroughly focused on the present, without the awareness of time passing
- Intrinsically motivated, meaning that doing the activity is its own reward

This type of rich experience has been called *flow*.[33] Much research has been done to understand the experience of flow and to help people achieve it in the area of sports. Many top athletes recognize the critical importance of being in the state of flow in order to perform at peak levels. Understanding flow in sports provides several important lessons that you can use as you think about finding flow at work. First, flow is not the same as pure pleasure; pleasure does not involve a sense of achievement or active contribution to the result, while flow does. Therefore, don't look only for something you enjoy, look for something that also gives you a sense of pride and accomplishment.

Second, flow occurs only when the challenge you face is in balance with your skills. Work that is far too difficult can cause anxiety; work that is far too easy leads quickly to boredom. Flow is a paradoxical kind of condition in which you're operating on a fine line where you can just (barely) do what needs to be done.[34] Look for work that stretches your abilities but does not make you feel overwhelmed.[35]

Energy

Tapping into multiple sources of energy is another analogy for being fully engaged. Great athletes, of course, achieve maximum performance by harnessing not only physical energy but also mental, emotional, and, for many, spiritual energy.[36] The same is true for people who excel at their work. Consider looking for work that will tap all your energy resources.

Thinking of engagement in this way is a reminder of three important elements that need to be part of any successful work experience, all of which relate to how you will build and manage your energy capacity as part of your work routines. Plugging in at peak engagement is not something that happens naturally, without practice. And it's not something you can do endlessly, with no opportunities to recharge. This energy analogy reminds us that full engagement:

1. Requires that energy "investments" be balanced with energy "deposits." As you tap into your individual energy, your supply is inevitably drawn down. You'll need to rebuild your energy supplies when they are low. This means that your periods of full engagement need to be offset by periods of strategic disengagement to restore the energy you've expended.

2. Requires that people push beyond normal limits, training like an elite athlete every day. Look for work that will allow you to challenge yourself a bit more each day. However, just as in physical exercise, the more you exceed your normal limits, the longer your recovery time will be.

3. Benefits from positive rituals and precise behaviors that become automatic over time. Think about the way elite athletes often rely on rituals, from how they manage their emotions under stress to the sort of mental-preparation routines they develop. For example, golfers often go through exactly the same steps before each putt. At work, rituals should focus on *doing* rather than not doing; an example of a positive ritual is, "I will check my e-mail at three specific times a day," rather than "I will stop checking my e-mail so often."

Our ability to engage is never endless. Based on your deepest values, beliefs, and preference, what work *deserves* to get your full engagement?

Your Personal Life Lures

The characteristics of work experiences that will create flow and tap your energy are what I call your *life lures*. Homing in on your personal lures should usefully serve as the basis for your choices about what work and where to work.

Use worksheet 4-2 to reflect on specific situations in your past in which you have felt the ways described in each line of the exercise "Remember a time when . . .?" Describe each situation in as much detail as possible. Were you . . .

- Working with a team, with one other person, or on your own?
- Doing something that you were winning at, that was directly benefiting others, that was fun?
- Engaging in something that you knew how to do well and for which the outcome was reasonably predictable, or inventing as you went along, doing something that involved some high-stakes risk?

What other descriptors of the experience stand out in your mind? Make notes on this exercise; use it to collect your ideas.

Keep in mind those situations you identified in which you felt highly engaged or passionate; the next step is to identify the practical characteristics of your ideal relationship with work and the pragmatic clues that will help you find it. There is a high correlation between certain types of passion, certain life lures, and specific, *identifiable* elements of the work environment. For example, someone with a passion for creating unique items with lasting value, let's say by writing books, is much more likely to prefer flexible schedules and independence than someone whose passion is leading teams successfully into competition.

My colleagues' and my research has identified six fundamentally different *archetypes* of work-related passions and preferred relationships

WORKSHEET 4-2

Remember a time when . . . : The characteristics of times when *you* were engaged

Remember a time . . .	What exactly was I doing?	What were the characteristics of the situation?
When you were excited and enthusiastic about something you were doing		
When you "lost yourself"—forgetting about time and place—as you did something		
When you resisted distractions for a significant period of time		
When you invested discretionary effort to produce significantly more than the task required, working all kinds of hours to get things done and done right		
When you found the challenge so inherently interesting that you pondered it happily even when you weren't directly engaged in it—perhaps in the car on the way home or in the morning shower		
When you developed creative new ways to do the work or searched for ways to improve things rather than just reacting to an obvious approach		
When you volunteered for the more difficult assignment		
When you were contagious, meaning you shared your enthusiasm with others in ways that encouraged them to join in, when you "recruited" others to the activity		
When you proudly identified with the activity and told others that this was what you did		

with work.[37] They describe the six roles that work plays in our lives today and represent six life lures.

- *Expressive legacy*—Work is most enjoyable when you are creating something with lasting value.

- *Secure progress*—Work is most enjoyable when you are feel you are on a predictable, upward path to success.
- *Individual expertise and team victory*—Work is most enjoyable when your expertise allows you to be a valuable member of a winning team.
- *Risk with reward*—Work is most enjoyable when you're taking a bit of risk, facing challenge and change, and learning with the possibility of wealth.
- *Flexible support*—Work is most enjoyable when it doesn't demand too much of you, when you can do it on a schedule that fits with your other life priorities.
- *Limited obligations*—Work is not particularly enjoyable; its value is largely its near-term economic gain.

Assess the ten statements in worksheet 4-3. Which of the statements in each row do you identify with *most* closely? Once you've completed the assessment, turn to table 4-1, "Your life lure perferences," to see which lures are most important to you.

The following descriptions of each lure will help you evaluate your current work. Some of the criteria apply to the actual nature of the tasks you may perform, and others apply to the work environment—the values of the organization, the management style of the boss, and so on. Is your current position the right one for you?

Expressive Legacy

Individuals who identify closely with this archetype tend to have the following characteristics:

- They care about building something with lasting value.
- They are entrepreneurial, hardworking, creative, well educated, and self-motivated.

WORKSHEET 4-3

What engages you?

Which of the statements do you identify with most *closely? Select the box or boxes that most closely match your preferences or feelings about work.*

	A	B	C	D	E	F
I like performing tasks when . . .	. . . the task itself is ambiguous and I personally need to figure out both what it might become and how to do it	. . . the approach for doing the task well has been determined by others and taught to me	. . . my team collectively possesses the skill and knowledge to perform the task, although I may only know one piece	. . . how to do the task is unknown and open-ended, requiring that we pioneer new approaches	. . . how to do the task well is clear and easy to learn	. . . the task is easy
I prefer work arrangements that . . .	. . . allow me complete individual latitude	. . . are well-defined and "traditional" (9 to 5)	. . . include regular hours that align the schedules of all team members and promote face time	. . . are highly flexible in terms of both time and place and provide time to pursue external adventures	. . . allow me to shift my schedule on a daily basis, as needed to balance my other responsibilities	. . . are short term
I like work that is . . .	. . . extremely stimulating, requiring creativity and providing opportunity to learn and grow	. . . challenging, but within my current capabilities based on the training I've received	. . . builds on my area of expertise and allows me to contribute my competence for collective good	. . . is extremely challenging and varied—and never involves doing the same thing twice	. . . is straightforward and has well-defined routines that I can plug in and out of, with others picking up where needed	. . . doesn't involve a lot of dumb questions from customers or colleagues
One of the things I would consider about a possible new employer is	. . . whether it would provide me with a platform for self-realization and the freedom to be entrepreneurial	. . . the quality of the long-term career development options—whether they represent a steady predictable path to success	. . . the extent to which my area of competence would contribute to the organization's success	. . . the opportunity for personal financial upside through bonus and stock	. . . the degree to which it would be possible to establish highly flexible arrangements including, preferably, self-scheduling	. . . whether the hiring process is quick and easy—with few required qualifications

WORKSHEET 4-3 (continued)

A deal breaker for me in selecting a job would be if	. . . I wouldn't be empowered to do the best work possible in the way I think it needs to be done	. . . the compensation philosophy didn't seem fair, including retirement benefits you can count on	. . . the environment did not promote collaboration and teamwork	. . . the deal did not offer the possibility of significant upside compensation	. . . . the deal did not include generous vacation policies and cafeteria-style benefits so I could get the type of support I most need	. . . it did not offer me a higher wage than the company down the street
I feel I am successful in my work if	. . . I am being true to myself, expressing myself by doing something I feel is of value	. . . I am making steady progress up the career ladder and saving for retirement	. . . my team wins and I have made a contribution to our shared success	. . . I am always learning and growing through exciting new assignments	. . . my activities outside work don't suffer, since they are currently far more important than this job	. . . the boss singles me out for a spot bonus because of something I did today
I get really psyched by . . .	. . . opportunities to build or create something with lasting value	. . . being on a steady road to success, with training and development along the way	. . . having fun with my colleagues—working hard together and celebrating	. . . interacting with really bright people and recognized thought leaders	. . . dreaming of how I'll plunge into work later in life, when my current external responsibilities are lessened	. . . a paycheck with some overtime or a bonus payment
In my life, work . . .	. . . is my opportunity to have a lasting impact on someone or something	. . . is my route to upward mobility and economic security	. . . is a major source of pride; based on our winning track record and my contributions to the team's success	. . . is an adrenaline rush—one of multiple opportunities for adventure and thrills	. . . is less important to me at the moment than my other responsibilities and interests	. . . honestly, a hassle.
It is important to me to have a manager who . . .	. . . helps me line up the resources I need for my work, leaves me alone to do it, keeps the bureaucrats away, and "promotes" my work when it's complete	. . . is clear and up-front with expectations, ties my compensation to fair goals, respects my tenure, and follows through on promises	. . . knows how to create a strong team, resolves any interpersonal conflicts quickly and competently, and acts as a player/coach to get the job done successfully	. . . lets me do new things based on my interests, treats me like an individual, gets rid of incompetent colleagues, and knows how to have fun	. . . understands that life is complicated for me now, is empathetic and willing to help me arrange a flexible schedule, but sees my longer-term potential	. . . is competent, fair, and pays me for the work I do
It is important to me to work for an organization that . . .	. . . does work that creates things of lasting value or that have social significance	. . . is financially stable and secure	. . . is known for its excellence and wins in the marketplace	. . . is "hot" and carries to the possibility of significant financial upside	. . . values its employees and has a caring employee value proposition	. . . pays well and isn't full of jerks

- They consider themselves leaders and love to assume responsibility.
- They are the most likely to define success as being true to themselves.
- They say they will never retire.
- They place less value on traditional rewards, such as compensation, vacation time, or a better benefits package than many others do.
- They are looking for work that continues to empower and stimulate them, enables them to continue to learn and grow, and has a greater social purpose.

If you share the values of this archetype, use the following criteria to judge the work you're doing and the work environment you're in today:

- *Individual latitude*—Do you have the ability to "be your own boss"?
- *Creativity-based success*—Is creativity required in order to excel at this work?
- *Ongoing opportunities to learn and grow*—Are you continually exposed to bright colleagues, stimulating ideas, and leading-edge issues?
- *Impact and sustained value*—Will your work have a lasting impact on someone or something?

Examples of the type of work that is often engaging for individuals in this archetype include architecture (creating something with lasting value), construction (individual latitude and lasting value), professional services (stimulating work, impact, and latitude), and many of the arts. Many individuals who are drawn to nonprofit work and social entrepreneurship are driven by this lure. In general, attractive work environments often include self-employment and entrepreneurial start-ups.

If you feel that expressive legacy is one of your dominant lures, you need to be involved in work that provides you with the satisfaction of creating, building, or doing work that helps others. You need to be part of an organization that places high priority on the nature of the work itself and on creating something with lasting value, often things that strongly reflect the company's heritage, values, and ambitions in unique and memorable ways. Bright Horizons, a provider of employer-sponsored child care, emphasizes the lasting impact an "early childhood educator" can have on young lives. A walk through Xilinx's hall of patents and past the mural depicting the founders' early vision for programmable logic devices leaves any visitor with a sense of the firm's compelling ambition.

Secure Progress

Individuals in this archetype have the following characteristics:

- They seek upward mobility and a steady, predictable path to success.
- They pride themselves on being highly reliable and loyal workers.
- They value fair, traditional rewards, including concrete compensation, good benefits, and a solid, predictable retirement package.
- They are uncomfortable with risky or highly variable compensation, including stock and bonuses.
- They like to work hard.
- They place high value on their family.
- They have less interest in "softer" work benefits like stimulating work, enjoyable workplaces, work that is worthwhile to society, or flexible work arrangements.
- They seek stable and secure environments and tend to have long tenures with one employer.

If you share the values of this archetype, it's important that you work for an organization that is able to provide:

- *Fair, concrete rewards*—Is the majority of your compensation based on either salary or an hourly wage, as opposed to incentive pay?

- *Predictable compensation, benefits, and a solid retirement package*—Are you able to predict what you'll earn each year and what you'll have available for retirement?
- *Stable, secure work environments*—Is the company's financial history and outlook sound? Does the company appear to be on a successful, sustainable path?
- *Work with structure and routine*—Does your role provide a regular routine and well-defined assignments?
- *Career-related training*—Do you have access to regular on-the-job training?

Examples of careers that are often engaging for individuals in this archetype include those in education, health care, government, manufacturing, and transportation.

Look for companies with a commitment to predictable rewards and investments in employee development. ExxonMobil made the decision to stick with defined benefit pension plans several years ago, recognizing the importance security played in its employees' experience. The Container Store's investment in training—more than five times the industry average—and clearly articulated progressions emphasize its strong commitment to career development.

Individual Expertise and Team Victory

Individuals in this archetype have the following characteristics:

- They enjoy being part of a winning team and seek a cooperative atmosphere.
- They care deeply about being highly competent at the work they do and contributing to the organization's success.
- They take pride in their work and are willing to put in extra effort.
- They are loyal, hardworking, reliable, capable, and typically very experienced.

- They place less value than most on individual rewards such as more money or vacation and express less need for flexible work arrangements.
- They place strong emphasis on personally stimulating work, congenial and fun work environments, cooperative colleagues, and employers that provide stability and job security.

If you share the values of this archetype, consider whether your current work provides:

- *Team-based work*—Do you have the opportunity to work closely with colleagues? Does the success of your work depend on the team's collective efforts?
- *Fun*—Do you take time out to enjoy the workday?
- *Approaches that are designed for collaboration*—Do your tasks require interaction with others?
- *Stable, well-organized, and well-run environments*—Does your organization have a successful and sustainable approach?
- *Competent colleagues*—Are your colleagues capable?
- *Work that leverages and builds your existing personal strengths*—Are you learning?

The particular industry is less important to individuals in this archetype than is finding team-based work environments. Many seek managerial roles.

Look for firms whose operating model requires team-based behavior. Royal Bank of Scotland is well known for its morning management meetings, in which every day's goals are set collaboratively by the top executives. Whole Foods's hiring and compensation processes are team-based; candidates are on probation until the team votes to hire them full time.

Risk with Reward

Individuals in this archetype have the following characteristics:

- They seek lives filled with change and adventure and see work as one of multiple opportunities to experience a thrill.
- They tend to be well educated and have a strong preference for working with other bright people.
- They thrive on exciting work.
- They enjoy assuming positions of responsibility.
- They are driven by variety and opportunities for growth.
- They want work that is inherently worthwhile.
- They pioneer new ways of working.
- They want flexible workplaces and schedules that enable them to work on their own terms and pursue their own interests.
- They are confident in their abilities and seek out bonus compensation and stock as rewards for their accomplishments.
- They own their careers and actively explore their career options; their tenures with employers are, on average, brief.

If you share the values of this archetype, consider whether your current position offers:

- *Personal financial upside*—Do you have the opportunity to receive substantial bonuses and stock as a result of your personal performance?
- *Flexible workplaces and schedules*—Is your work based on your own terms?
- *Opportunities to choose assignments*—Can you choose from a wide menu of options?

- *Opportunities to change tasks frequently*—Do you have the option of shifting responsibilities?
- *Open-ended tasks*—Are you able to define the approach?
- *Frequent exposure to other bright people and recognized thought leaders*—Does your work bring you in contact with people you respect and learn from?

Examples of work environments that can be engaging for individuals who fit the risk-with-reward archetype include those in information technology, investment banking, and professional services. Many of these individuals are frequently happiest working for smaller organizations or being self-employed. Trilogy, a software firm, has a highly challenging orientation process in order to create this culture from the start.

Flexible Support

Individuals in this archetype have the following characteristics:

- They see work as a source of livelihood but not as a primary focus in their lives.
- They are typically pursuing interests and priorities outside of work and are trying to balance their lives personally, financially, and emotionally.
- They are looking for employers that can make it a little easier to cope, for example, by offering a flexible menu of benefit options that fit their specific needs.
- They value congenial and fun environments.
- They tend to view their nonwork activities as temporary and think they may want to devote more time and energy to their work in the future, but for now are seeking roles at work that will enable them to control both their careers and lives.

If you share the values of this archetype, you need to be in a work environment that offers:

- *Highly flexible work arrangements*—Can you create your own schedule?
- *Generous vacation or options for leave*—Do you have the option to take off significant periods of time?
- *Flexible benefit programs*—Can you choose among childcare, elder care, and other options based on your specific needs?
- *Work with well-defined routines*—Do you have the ability to plug in and out again with ease?
- *Work that can be done virtually*—Can your work be done without direct personal interaction?
- *Work environments that are congenial, empathetic, and fun*—Do you enjoy your boss and colleagues?

Examples of work environments that are often engaging for individuals in this archetype include leisure and hospitality or financial services, since both are often able to offer the flexibility this group desires. JetBlue's system for its reservation agents allows them to work at home and self-schedule within their work group, an example of competing for talent on the basis of maximum flexibility. But a growing number of organizations in other industries recognize the importance of flexibility in the workplace, so you are likely to find a lot, if not all, of these features in practically every field.

Limited Obligations

Individuals who fit the limited-obligations profile have the following characteristics (although given these characteristics, they're probably not reading this book!):

- They see the value of work largely in terms of near-term economic gain.

- They prefer work that makes minimal demands on their time.
- They place high value on traditional compensation and benefits packages.
- They express less interest than other profiles in work that is enjoyable, personally stimulating, or worthwhile to society.

If you share the values of this archetype, you'll be happiest if your employment has:

- *Low barriers to entry*—Was the hiring process quick and easy and the job relatively easy to come by and learn?
- *Work with well-defined routines*—Is the preferred approach clearly outlined?
- *Traditional compensation and lucrative benefits packages*—Is your compensation based primarily on salary or hourly wage?
- *Stability and security*—Does the company have a good track record for financial and strategic stability?
- *Opportunities for periodic recognition*—Is it possible to receive rewards for strong contributions?

Examples of work environments that might be best suited to individuals in this archetype, largely because the positions have low barriers to entry, include retail, wholesale, and transportation.[38]

Are you in a situation in which you have a realistic shot at enjoying your work, if you don't today? Or do you need to face the challenge of moving to something or somewhere else as you position yourself for the next phase of your career?

Use the criteria associated with your life lure to reflect on how you feel about the work you're doing today and the environment in which you're doing it. If you don't get this part right, no matter what strategies you employ to become more successful, you almost certainly won't be *engaged*. And, without engagement, success on your terms will be an elusive prey.[39]

TABLE 4-1

Your life lure preferences

Your life lure preferences are as follows:

Column A	*Expressive legacy*: Work is about creating something with lasting value.
Column B	*Secure progress*: Work is about upward mobility; a predictable, upward path to success.
Column C	*Individual expertise and team victory*: Work is an opportunity to be a contributing member of a winning team.
Column D	*Risk with reward*: Work is an opportunity for challenge, change, learning, and, maybe, wealth.
Column E	*Flexible support*: Work generates a livelihood but not currently a life priority.
Column F	*Limited obligations*: Work's value is largely its near-term economic gain.

CHAPTER FIVE

A Hard Look at the Options Ahead

The Reality of the Changing Workplace

The nature and availability of work is changing in important ways, ways that will significantly affect the opportunities open to Generation X over the upcoming decades. And most of the news is good. Despite near-term job shortages, the longer-term outlook for work is promising. The trend is toward tighter labor markets, providing you greater leverage to find the work you want. Better still, the nature of work, spurred by continuing changes in technology, promises opportunities that are more closely aligned with your values and with the types of lives you hope to lead.

The Availability of Work

Here's a simple way to think about the long-term talent situation: many economies around the globe are reaching sizes that provide the *capacity* to create more jobs than the projected working age population can fill.

(This assumes we continue to define *working age* as we currently do: those between eighteen and sixty-five years of age, which I'll discuss later.) Without question, over the past several decades, birth rates have slowed, while, until the past year, economies continued to grow.

In the United States, birth rates have fallen from the three-plus children per two adults in the 1950s and 1960s to just over two children for every two adults in the 2000s. In other words, we are just about replacing ourselves. Because birth rates have been low for several decades now, as those children enter the workforce over the next twenty years, the size of the U.S. workforce will grow *very* slowly, by less than half a percent per year. To put that in context, from 1980 to 2000, the number of people in the twenty-five to fifty-four age group, historically the prime source of the nation's workforce, increased by 35 million in the United States. From 2000 to 2020, it will grow by just 3 million.[1]

Meanwhile, over the past several decades, the economy has boomed. Companies have grown, and although the nature of the jobs available has shifted, the number has steadily increased. Before the recession of 2008, the economy was so big that it was poised to create more jobs than the traditionally defined workforce could fill.

This phenomenon—slowing birth rates in the face of growing economies—is happening around the world as local economies shift from agrarian-based to industry-based to knowledge-based jobs. Here's the straightforward connection. In an agrarian economy, children represent labor. More children allow families to produce more crops. Kids are *assets*. In industrial and professional service economies, the impact of children on the family changes. In these economies, kids cost money. They are *liabilities*. There's no question they're loved and valued, but for most couples in an industrial or knowledge-based economy, one or two will do. Children have shifted on the balance sheet of life. As a result, as economies around the world continue to evolve, birth rates will almost certainly continue to fall.

Today, the highest fertility rate in the world—7.3 children per woman—is in Mali, where the key industry is agriculture and, specifically, cotton (an extremely labor-intensive crop). On the other end of the spectrum, the lowest birth rates in the world are found in Asia (South Korea, 1.2; Taiwan and Singapore, 1.1; Hong Kong, 1.0; and Macau, 0.9), where service-based economies centered on finance and tourism dominate.

As economies around the world continue to evolve, birth rates will almost certainly continue to fall. The European Union average in 2008 was 1.5; countries like Italy and Spain were at 1.3, significantly below replacement levels. Europe's working-age population will actually *decline* in size over future decades. In the European Union, the workforce (individuals between fifteen and sixty-four) will shrink by over 15 percent or 52 *million* workers between 2004 and 2050.[2]

Bottom line: There are likely to be plenty of jobs for you in the future as economies rebound from the current dip.

There are, of course, several sensitivities to this forecast. Although none of these are likely to diminish the prospects for jobs at a macro level, they definitely create disruption, imbalance, and significant pain in the pockets affected.

Boomer Retirements

What if Boomers don't stop working when they reach retirement age? The preceding statistics assume that the workforce ends with those aged sixty-five, but we are already seeing evidence that people are working later in life. Over the next decade, I expect to see official retirement ages increase as more individuals choose to remain in the workforce.

However, most Boomers don't want to work as long or as hard once they reach this post-sixty-five period. Almost all say they want to cut back or work on a more flexible basis. Even if you make some pretty aggressive assumptions about the number of older Americans who remain active, there will still be gaps in the workforce and top jobs opening up for you.

Outsourcing

Outsourcing has been particularly painful for your generation. Wage levels for men have been declining over the past several decades. One cause has been the movement of high-wage jobs traditionally dominated by men—manufacturing jobs—to other countries. Also, a disproportionately high percentage of your generation went to work in information technology–related sectors, another segment of the economy that has been particularly vulnerable to outsourcing.

However, global sourcing has limitations, and there are signs that the trend is slowing. Wages are rising quickly in these recipient economies, and competition for qualified candidates is fierce.[3] Many companies are reevaluating the trade-offs and electing to keep a higher proportion of their jobs in developed economies or even bringing some of the jobs home. And even if every job that could possibly be done in a physically distant location were outsourced, labor shortages would still exist in developed countries. Although competition from global labor markets will continue downward pressure on domestic wages and individuals may need to retrain or relocate within the country, there will be jobs available in the United States and other developed economies.

Immigration

Generation X has also been significantly affected by immigration. First, a significant percentage of you are immigrants. Nineteen percent of twenty-five- to thirty-nine-year-olds in the United States in 2004 were born outside the United States, compared with only 12 percent of the population overall. Of those, nearly half were from Central America, including Mexico, and a quarter from Asia. Today, only 26 percent of you in this age group who were foreign born have become naturalized citizens.[4] Looked at another way, 40 percent of all legal immigrants admitted into the United States in 2004 were between the ages of twenty-five and thirty-nine.[5]

Immigration is of concern to those who feel that domestic jobs are being lost to lower-cost immigrant labor. But this trend also has limitations, for two reasons. As population growth rates slow around the world, fewer people will be available to emigrate. Poland, for example, has been a major source of immigrant labor into the United Kingdom, but today it has one of the lowest birth rates in the world. Growth in the

Mexican working-age population will slow tenfold, from a 200 percent increase during the forty years from 1970 to 2010 to only a 20 percent increase from 2010 to 2050. Recent reports suggest that the flow of illegal immigrants from Mexico into the United States slowed dramatically in 2008, a trend that in all likelihood will continue over the years ahead.[6] As shown in figure 5-1, the growth rate of working-age populations is slowing dramatically in many countries.

The second factor is that the attractiveness of many local economies is rapidly improving, causing individuals to choose to remain or return home.

Productivity

Even technology, with the promise of robots and other labor-saving devices, is unlikely to reduce the number of jobs available for you. Productivity in the United States has increased an average of about 2 percent per year over the past fifty years. Most economists believe the overall long-term rate will hold steady during the decades ahead.

The Near-Term Economy

Just your luck, the economy was slow when you entered the workforce and now it's slowing once again, just as you are standing at the threshold of senior management. As I write this, the global economy is going through a difficult cycle. The unemployment rate in the United States is higher than it has been in twenty-six years. I didn't discuss the near-term economy in my previous two books on the generations and won't in detail here. From a demographic perspective, the long-term demand for labor should be robust. But it may take several years for us to climb out of the current conditions and resume an economic growth trajectory; thus, some of the leverage that individuals will have in the workforce will likely take some additional time to materialize.

The implications of the current economy vary by generation. But whether through shrinking retirement savings, fewer first jobs, or widespread midcareer layoffs, all generations are feeling the pinch.

FIGURE 5-1

Slower growth in the working-age population

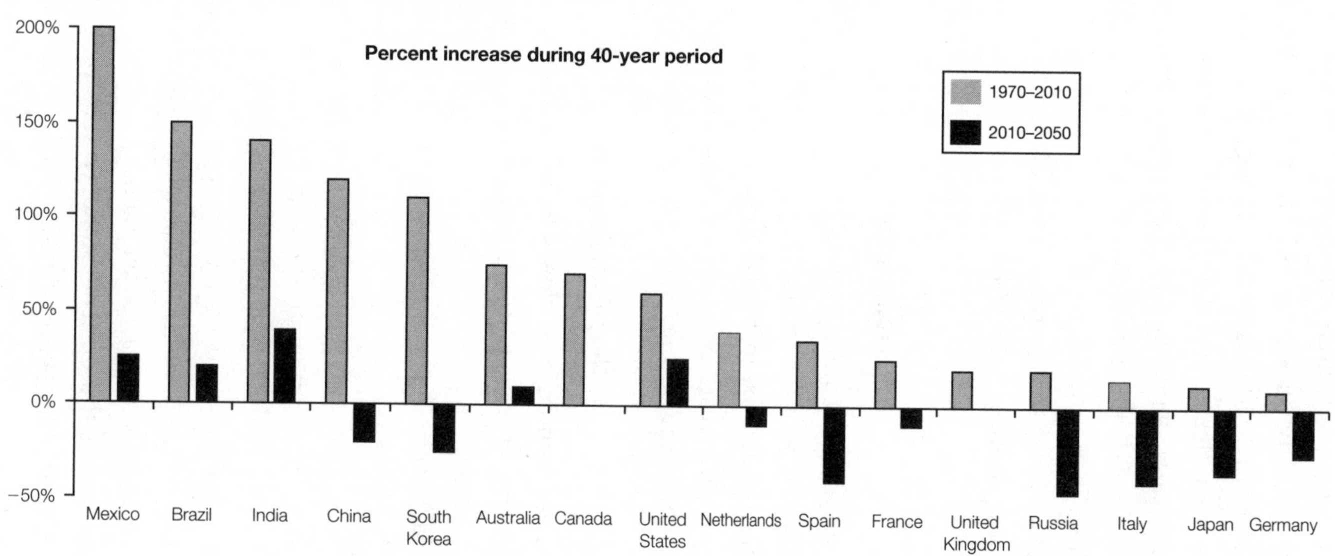

Source: "It's 2008: Do You Know Where Your Talent Is? Why Acquisition and Retention Strategies Don't Work," Deloitte Research/U.N. Population Division (http://esa.un.org/unpp/), 6.

Y's are probably the least affected. Despite a slowdown in immediate career opportunities, the current financial crisis is unlikely to diminish the long-term fortunes of this generation. They can afford to create a short-term strategy to make the best of a difficult economic time, with the expectation of a long life in which to ride the investment cycle back up.

The recession has reset the game board for Boomers. Options for full retirement that appeared viable twelve months ago are now off the table for many. The reality, however, is that few Boomers were headed for an old-time, no-work version of retirement, even before the recession. Most will need to work postretirement, but will be able to meet their financial obligations through reduced work commitments, and still fulfill many of their other interests.

Of the three major generations in the workplace today, Generation X is almost certainly facing the most difficult challenge. As I've discussed, many X'ers are carrying significant financial burdens—old school loans, mortgage payments, child-care expenses, and other adult responsibilities. For many of you, this recessionary period is likely to feel like sailing through choppy seas in a heavily laden boat, with little freeboard to withstand major waves.

There's a natural inclination to hunker down—lie low and keep out of sight—as you attempt to remain gainfully employed during a time when layoffs will almost certainly continue to be a day-to-day reality in many organizations. Paradoxically, that is unlikely to be the best approach. Usually, the best approach in difficult times is to step forward—to lean into the challenge. In later chapters, I'll offer ideas to take full advantage of the changing nature of work to bring innovative ideas and new ways of doing things to your organization.

The Nature of Work

The basis of our economy—the way we create value—has been changing for centuries, from agrarian to manufacturing to service-based work. Today *knowledge work*, a specialized segment of the service economy, makes up an estimated 40 percent of American jobs and accounts for 70 percent of job growth since 1998.[7]

Your generation's jobs reflect the swing toward a service-dominated economy. The highest proportion are in retail and government services (11 percent of you work in each area), followed closely by information technology and other services (10 percent each), health services (9 percent), and education (8 percent). Your job patterns are very different from those of members of other generations, particularly in manufacturing, where only 6 percent of you are employed, compared with 10 percent of the Boomers. This shift in the underlying job patterns will continue around the world throughout the remainder of your working years, enabled by technological advances.

Drivers of Change

The primary drivers of the changing nature of work are straightforward: technology increasingly allows what people in the workplace would probably always have preferred—greater influence and increased flexibility. During the past ten years, a number of new technologies (which X'ers have been largely responsible for creating) have substantially altered the way we do many things by reducing the costs of communication.

Your voices

We have reached [this stage of] development because of Gen X'ers—because of their enterprise, and because of their willingness to do an end run around the dominant modes of communication. What's both inspiring and disorienting about this brave new world is that X'ers invented the template for it.[8]

Some of the major technological advances include:

- *Anywhere, anytime access*—Widely available, inexpensive connections providing ubiquitous communication around the world

- *Information you want when you need it*—Easy-to-use approaches for organizing and identifying knowledge
- *Practical sharing of knowledge and ideas*—Quick and easy ways to form relationships and conduct work
- *The ability to test ideas*—Online services that allow experimentation without high investment costs

These changes redistribute knowledge and, in doing so, shift power. One of the great thinkers on the power of knowledge was Harold Adams Innis. In *The Bias of Communication*, a groundbreaking work published in 1951, Innis explains that breaking down the monopoly on knowledge has predictable consequences, including:

- Making it easier for "amateurs" to compete with "professionals," because access to knowledge substitutes for mastery of complexity.
- Allowing individuals and minorities to voice ideas, as the media becomes accessible to all.
- Reducing the advantages of speed that formerly accrued because some had knowledge before others.
- Reducing the advantages of size that are based on the ability to afford high costs.[9]

New Forms of Value Creation

Today, the emergent information-based economy is evolving into something even more powerful and distinct. You can feel it happening—for example, in Barack Obama's participative election campaign, in YouTube's amateur video production and distribution capabilities, and in Wikipedia's collective input. We're in the midst of a fundamental, disruptive, technology-driven shift in how markets, businesses, and societies function.

The exact outlines and possibilities will continue to be shaped over the years ahead, but we are moving to what we might call a *choice economy*, characterized by individuals' ability to participate directly and exercise choice—to customize, cocreate, and collaborate. Umair Haque, director of the Havas Media Lab, calls this new world the *edge economy*, arguing, as Innis did over a half-century ago, that as knowledge shifts, value is created at the edge by people who previously did not have the power to participate fully.[10]

Whatever it's called, the way businesses create value is changing, essentially in ways that are more closely aligned with X'er preferences and sensibilities. For example:

- *Through investments in individual experience*—As communication costs drop, the shorthand of logos and slogans becomes unnecessary; individuals can access information on costs and benefits in rich detail. Increasingly, brand value is created by and embodied in the experiences of millions of users. The shift echoes X'er sensibilities: less emphasis on being told what you should know or believe, more on alternatives that respect individual input and choice.

- *By cutting through obfuscation*—This is another major X'er value. Everyone's activities are becoming more transparent. As the cost of communication goes toward zero, it becomes increasingly likely that *what goes around, comes around.* Unfairly achieving short-term advantage is more likely to result in longer-term negative consequences. High ethical standards will be good for business.

- *Through a strategy of "lessness"*—Echoing a classic X'er value, 37signals, a fast-growing software company, is committed to "one-down" the competition and "under-do" its rivals. Rather than launching products with more features, 37signals succeeds through a strategy of lessness by offering products that are refreshing models of simplicity in an industry ruled by complexity.[11]

- *By allowing others to play*—Decreasing the cost of communication facilitates the creation of networks. In network economics, the most successful systems are those that allow others to play.

In popular peer-to-peer systems, producers apply open source principles to create products made of bits—from operating systems to encyclopedias.[12] Prosumer communities give customers the tools they need to participate in value creation.[13]

- *Through organization*—Markets, networks, and communities can be used to manage resources and ideas more efficiently, if a fabric of incentives for sustainable growth and authentic value creation is part of the design. Google says its goal is to "organize the world's information."[14] Muhammad Yunus revolutionized finance and created social transformation, not by collecting more money to lend, but by using the organizing power of communities to alter the value equation of lending to the poor.[15] *Ideagoras* are networks that organize brain power, giving companies access to a global marketplace of ideas, innovations, and uniquely qualified minds that they can use to extend their problem-solving capacity.[16]

Business strategies—the ways value will be created—will become more X-like. What about the organizations?

The Nature of Organizations

By the quarter-mark of this century, successful, sustainable organizations will evolve into connected communities encompassing a wide variety of partners and contractor relationships. Participants will be intensely collaborative, continually informed, technologically adept, and skilled at ongoing experimentation. Unconstrained by rigid boundaries, the communities will tap regional "hot spots" around nodes of connectivity, talent, and infrastructure.[17] Work will increasingly be done anywhere, anytime, rather than in fixed locations on nine-to-five schedules.

These trends will change the work opportunities you will have over the next several decades. Companies will adopt flexible relationships and continuous active connections to attract both talented employees and loyal customers. Organizations will struggle to operate on a more human scale, while creating robust and agile enterprises with the built-in capacity for innovation, sustained growth, and global operation.

The new direction represents a significant departure from the typical features of today's corporations, all of which serve to create stability *for the institution*:

- Traditional organizations focus individuals on doing a predefined task.
- The established product or service becomes the overriding determinant of success.
- Standards and structures are assumed to be essential.
- Performance is measured against quantitative results based on defined standards.
- Reality is conceived of as dichotomous and competitive (success-failure, in-group–out-group, leader-follower, legitimate-illegitimate, work-play, reasonable-emotional).

These characteristics do not encourage ambiguity or change. They essentially serve to collude with the side of our personality that resists the contradictions that the evolution under way requires.

So why will things change? Because the underlying assumptions are no longer valid. And because you want them to.

The Old Assumptions

Most organizations today are based on assumptions that either are or soon will be no longer valid. For example, most of today's organizational principles are still centered on the premise that the workforce is shaped like a pyramid. There are a few people at the top (even more basically, there *is* a "top") making key decisions and setting strategy, a larger number of people in the middle who translate strategy into day-to-day operations, and a lot of workers at the bottom who are more or less doing as instructed. This model is the basis for a number of now-standard organizational practices. For example, employees are promoted (at least until they reach their Peter Principle level) in order to provide variety (something new and interesting to do) and increased compensation. This model is just fine, as long as the underlying pyramid-shaped population provides room for most people (who live long enough) to move up.

But today the workforce is not pyramidal. It is more like a diamond, with a large middle group, and it is rapidly evolving into a rectangle, with nearly the same number of workers at each major life stage. Going forward, many of our deeply ingrained assumptions about the course of a person's lifetime career will be *mathematically* impossible. The pyramid will not offer enough higher-level positions to provide everyone in the workforce with upward opportunities for variety, learning, or increased compensation, particularly as the generational cohorts become more eager for frequent change and less willing to remain in one position for extended periods of time.

Another example of shifting assumptions: if you overlay today's demographic patterns with the changing nature of value creation—the growth in knowledge-based, or even choice-based, edge-economy work—you can question whether our widely accepted parameters around time and job design continue to make sense. Most jobs today are still described in terms of units of time—a forty-hour workweek, an eight-hour day (if you're lucky enough to find an organization that doesn't stretch the laws of physics and turn eight hours a day into sixty or seventy hours a week!). But the majority of workers in the Western world are now employed in service industries, and already more than half of those are knowledge workers, paid for writing, analyzing, advising, counting, designing, researching, and countless related functions, including capturing, organizing, and providing access to knowledge used by others. Time-based jobs make little sense for these workers. Who is to say how long it takes an individual to write a report, conduct an analysis, or produce a piece of software?

Through it all, your needs and values are changing. At some point, the tightening labor market will motivate even the most traditional companies to change or face the likelihood that their growth will be constrained by a lack of talent. At the core, the relationship between employees and employers—or perhaps more accurately, between workers and the organizers of work—will be redefined. These shifts will both reinforce and enable the desires of individual workers, allowing greater personal flexibility, autonomy, and participation.

Back from the Future—Getting from Here to There

A different type of enterprise, with an accelerated pace, intensive collaboration, and on-demand execution, will call out for different assumptions about the organizational structure and a different style of management.

Ricardo Semler, CEO of the innovative Brazilian company Semco, says,

> *Moving an organization or business ahead by virtue of what its people stand for and the deeds they do, means removing obstacles like official policies, procedural constraints, and relentless milestones, all of which are established to pursue quarterly or otherwise temporary success. It means giving up control, and allowing employees to manage themselves. It means trusting workers implicitly, sharing power and information, encouraging dissent, and celebrating true democracy. Few things are harder for managers, executives, shareholders and owners to embrace.*[18]

Umair Haque adds:

> *It requires a "leap of faith"—a major step of strategic imagination—to see and then believe in a vastly different, radically better future—and not be limited to seeing and believing in a grainy, washed-out future that seems depressingly inevitable . . . It takes a profound appetite for revolution: a profound ability to let go of yesterday's stale, tired, and thoroughly toxic orthodoxies—to explode the shrunken, stunted strategic imagination the industrial-era firm suffers from.*[19]

But, no matter the difficulty, change is happening, spurred by the values and preferences advocated by your generation, strongly supported by the Ys, and facilitated by technology that allows more networked, horizontal organizations and, with this, new ways to get work done.

What does such change mean for organizations and the arrangements between organizations and those who perform work? Here's a partial list of the changes I expect over the next fifteen years, many of which are already evident to some extent.

Innovation will be a key organizational capability. Organizations will increasingly require innovation to achieve business success. The implications will be apparent in new styles of leadership and new organizational designs, as I'll discuss further in chapter 8.

Strategy and long-range planning will disappear. Business will operate through continual experimentation and evaluation, allowing little time for lengthy planning and approval cycles. As this happens, responsibility for strategy will disperse throughout the enterprise.

Corporate success will be measured in metrics of sustainability. Performance metrics will be reevaluated in light of the financial disaster and other hard lessons of 2008. We may even come to question the importance of growth. As Jason Fried of 37signals reflects, "Revenue growth in and of itself is not a goal . . . There is a right size for certain things, at least if you want to do them well."[20] The effects of the organization on the environment (social accounting) will be incorporated into the way we evaluate corporate performance.

The notion of chain of command will break down. Because information, knowledge, and expertise will be widely and constantly shared, the traditional model of management geared to controlling a bureaucracy by sending a few key directives down through a deep hierarchy will disappear.

Many decisions will be made through participative or democratic processes. It has become both economically and logistically feasible to obtain input from large numbers of people and even to introduce voting or market-based mechanisms into the workplace. Increasingly, many individuals will have line-of-sight to the business results they influence and a voice in key decisions.

The role of managers will be to design and orchestrate systems that engage the participation of others. Managers will be less defined by their singular subject matter expertise than by their skill in eliciting input from many.

Data will not be secure. We will give up on this already out-of-date ideal and focus instead on engaging individuals in the enterprise who are trustworthy—adults who see their own best interests and the interests of the organization as aligned—and therefore are not motivated to destroy value.

Technology will be owned by individuals. Organizations will no longer supply personal technology, such as laptops and cell phones, because employees will already own them; the focus will shift to plugging them in. A close corollary is that workers will access external data—social networks and the blogosphere—as an integral part of the work experience.

High ethical standards will be an important predictor of sustained success. It will be more than okay to tell a customer that you've made an error or more broadly admit that you've screwed up.[21] Transparency will favor voluntary ethical behavior.

Units of work will be expressed and measured in terms of tasks, not time. Practical realities in the new economy encourage moving toward a task-based definition of jobs. It is difficult to quantify the time required for knowledge work: how long does it take to write, say, a piece of software? Employees will put in only as much time as it actually takes to get the work done. The distinction between full- or part-time positions will give way to differentiation in the complexity of the task assigned.

Flexible arrangements will be replaced by individual discretion. Rather than the managed options for variations in time and place available in most corporations, individuals will control when and where they work. Most work will occur asynchronously from multiple locations.

The concept of weekends will disappear. Organizations will no longer dictate the days an individual should or should not work. There will be no need for company-defined synchronous hours in most occupations.

Most physical meetings will be optional. Synchronous meetings will occur less frequently, and individuals will determine which would be beneficial to attend. Social networking tools will be widely used to gather input asynchronously.

We will work fewer hours. Already progressive companies are recognizing the benefits of working less. 37signals, which insists on fewer hours, recently adopted an official four-day workweek, the better to keep everyone fresh, energized, and forced to avoid distractions.[22] Happily, technology, and particularly the option of asynchronous input, will also make us more efficient, allowing these shorter hours.

Titles reflecting status will disappear. Today, titles serve two purposes. One is to identify to others (customers and colleagues within the organization) to whom they should look for specific actions or decisions. The other is to reflect our status in the organization. The first purpose will remain and become increasingly important. Collaboration occurs when responsibilities and roles are clearly defined. Titles that clarify the function the person performs—editor of the company newsletter, manager of the sales team, accountant for the West Coast operations—will be more essential than ever. But titles that recognize our progress in an organization will disappear because they cement us into a hierarchical structure that no longer serves our needs or, in some cases, even exists.

Classic staff functions will re-assume some of the responsibilities now being dispersed to line management roles. As the diversity of work arrangements grows—with some people working part-time, some cyclically, some as employees, some on a contract basis—and the need to juggle a wide variety of individuals with diverse preferences and needs intensifies, traditional line managers will happily pass the challenge of managing such a complicated talent pool back to a staff function. A talent management function, the next evolution of today's human resources, will become the home base for the corporation's workforce—attracting, tracking, developing, and orchestrating this complex talent corps. Like staffing managers in professional service firms today or talent agencies in the film industry, the talent management function will be judged on the quality, engagement, and readiness of the talent the business needs.

Line managers will function more like project managers. As the current movement to shift more people-management responsibility to line managers reverses, operating managers will focus on overseeing the deployment of talent, much as a director might in the film industry, setting direction for the team of employees who have been assigned to the task or division at that moment in time.

An individual's career will be neither continuous nor linear. Employees will leave and reenter the workforce, a phenomenon Sylvia Ann Hewett and Caroline Buck Luce have called "off-ramping" and "on-ramping."[23] Organizations will learn to accommodate this work pattern.

Retirement will no longer occur at a specific, common age. Already, 34 percent of all U.S. workers say they *never* plan to retire.[24] Extended life expectancies will also augur the end of orchestrated retirement as we have known it.

Career paths will lead down, as well as up. Rather than the cliff-shaped career paths of the past century in which individuals ascended on an upward path toward ever greater success, which ended abruptly with complete retirement, twenty-first century career paths will be bell-shaped. A career-deceleration phase for employees in their fifties through eighties will parallel the career development phase of the twenties through forties. (See figure 5-2.)

Older workers will work in entry-level jobs. As individuals choose to enter and exit the workforce at multiple times throughout their lives, in many cases pursuing multiple careers, older workers will be candidates for entry-level jobs that offer a way into new lines of work or flexible options suited to a preferred lifestyle.

Cyclic work will be the norm. Many individuals will choose to work in a contractor-like pattern—an intense period on, followed by an extended period off. Already a substantial proportion of workers of all ages say that they'd prefer this pattern if it were available to them.[25]

Employment will be a specialized subset of the relationships between workers and organizations. The relationships that the corporation will have with the people who perform work on its behalf will encompass a wide

FIGURE 5-2

The shape of careers to come

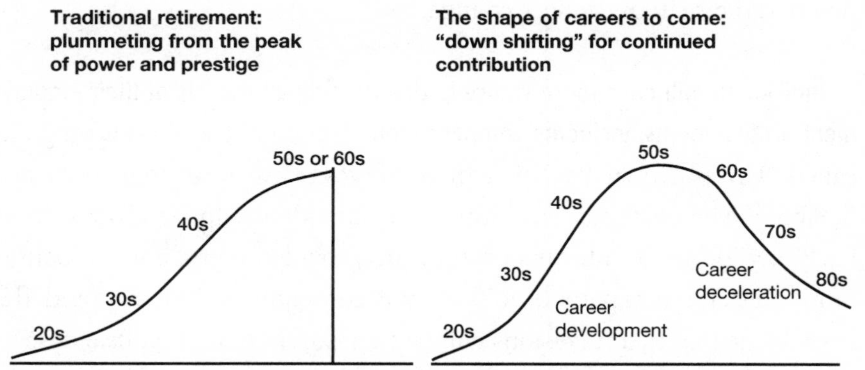

range—contractors, freelancers, small company specialists, outsourcers, and many others. The distinction between who is inside and who is external will blur.

Providing feedback will mean teaching, not evaluating. Once a year, sit-down reviews are already an anachronism. Managers will be expected to teach on an ongoing basis, rather than judge periodically. Mechanisms for frequent, peer-based input will be the norm.

Short tenure will be the expectation, rather than the exception. Jobs will be designed to assume frequent movement and short tenures. The time required to get up to speed to perform a specific function will be shortened.

Work arrangements will be fair, but customized, rather than equal. Organizations will structure unique arrangements suited to each individual's needs and preferences, recognizing the widely differing values and assumptions about work inherent in today's workforce. Deloitte & Touche, for example, has already substituted a corporate lattice for the traditional corporate ladder. Employees choose from a set of options to increase or decrease four aspects of work: how fast they progress toward promotion, how much they produce, the degree to which their hours and travel are restricted, and their level of responsibility, from individual contributor to leader. The goal is to allow individuals to step up, move laterally, or move down as their circumstances change.[26]

Individuals will have more choice in determining all aspects of their employment arrangements, including compensation. Semco already has a program called "Up 'n' Down Pay" in which employees manage their own pay flexibly.[27] The company has found that individuals almost always do so fairly, based on the information they are provided regarding compensation levels for comparable jobs in the company or industry and the knowledge that their decisions will be transparent to their colleagues.

A more subtle appreciation of diversity, particularly diversity around points of view, will increase. As complexity increases, successful leaders will be those who appreciate the rightness of multiple positions. (In many ways, one of the major goals of this book is to help explain why X'ers *are* right, and Boomers and Y's are as well, based on the events and ideas that shaped their lives.)

Corporations will be active participants and partners in education. Corporations already play an increasingly active role in creating a workforce with the skills and capabilities required for the evolving economy. Involvement will grow as more organizations find that the current educational system is not geared to produce a workforce matched to today's business needs.

Learning will be an integral part of work. We will recognize that learning is not something one does before one works; it is an ongoing part of the work process. Already we are shifting away from linear learning through authoritative sources to a process termed *bricolage*—pulling pieces of information from a variety of sources and piecing them together.

Companies will encourage employees to opt out if the fit is not right. Responsibility for choosing the right fit between worker and organization will increasingly be placed on the worker. When Zappos, the online shoe retailer, hires new customer service employees, it provides a four-week training period that immerses them in the company's strategy, culture, and obsession with customers. After a week in this immersive experience, the company offers the employees a $1,000 bonus if they agree to quit that day, driven by the logic that if you're willing to take the company up on the offer, you don't have the sense of commitment Zappos is looking for.[28] Zappos wants to learn if there's a bad fit between what makes the organization tick and what makes individual employees tick, and it's willing to pay to learn sooner rather than later. Increasingly, companies will find ways to let employees understand for themselves what it's like to work there, and then encourage the prospective employee to evaluate the fit.

Work processes will gather input from multiple sources. Work processes will be designed specifically to accept and benefit from inputs from multiple sources. The use of widespread collaboration in scientific research will lower costs and accelerate our pace of increased understanding. Platforms will invite the participation of developers and external partners to build tools or invent new applications. Manufacturing processes will leverage human capital across borders and organizational boundaries to design and assemble physical things. Workplaces will invite bottom-up innovation.

If the work arrangements that are available to you today don't include the ones you'd prefer, encourage the creation of a wider variety. (My coauthors and I discussed many of these types of arrangements in more detail in our book *Workforce Crisis*.)[29] If your organization is not leveraging new technology options for both the way you provide products and services, and the way you operate internally, take the lead in offering new ideas (chapter 6 offers concrete ideas for shaping the organization to fit you).

Implications for Where the Jobs Are

As you look for opportunities for your next fifty years of work, first look for businesses that are pursuing strategies based on the principles of a new economy: those that are open, transparent, and fair to all participants in the ecosystem and that *use* the capabilities technology now provides to organize markets, networks, and communities. These organizations are most likely to be found where there is the greatest need and therefore opportunity and the greatest motivation to change: areas of the economy that today are dominated by structural barriers to efficiency and productivity.[30] Much of the opportunity ahead lies in socially responsible arenas: energy, water, health, hunger, finance, and education. All of these are inefficient industries that cry out for new approaches.[31] But they're not alone. As Wikipedia has shown, even a very established product, the encyclopedia, can be completely upended through new-economy approaches.

No one knows for sure where tomorrow's jobs will lie. A few trends are obvious: opportunities in health care will be strong for the foreseeable future. Science and engineering, as well as government service, will be hit by Boomer retirements. Education in computer science fell so dramatically in the early 2000s that demand will outstrip supply in information technology going forward. But beyond these obvious trends, the real opportunity lies with your creativity, with Generation X's ability to tackle old problems in new ways.

Beyond the Corporation

Business, of course, is not the only area of occupation, and corporations are far from the only type of employer. If that's where you are, but you feel that it's time to move on, it's not too late to look at entirely different fields. You may already have transferable skills. If not, you have time to get them, even through part-time learning and training.

Here are a few other options in types of organizations or work that is changing.

Professional Services

The option of becoming a consultant or otherwise hanging out your own shingle in accounting, law, or other professions is a way to gain flexibility and independence, without the complications of a full entrepreneurial start-up. In addition, many professional service firms are beginning to offer a variety of more flexible career-path options that may allow you to find the balance you're looking for within the bounds of a larger firm.

Education

Education is being challenged to change and to strive for outcomes that are better matched to this century's job market. As Generation X ascends to greater civic and professional leadership, you are likely to exert increasing pressure for choice, accountability, transparency, and performance. With your influence, various bold entrepreneurial efforts may be created to reshape education.[32] A number of organizations have already been founded by Generation X social entrepreneurs to bring new, young blood into the educational system and create competition with the existing hierarchy.[33] For example:

- Teach For America (TFA), with its goal of bringing top performers into teaching, is perhaps the best known, and its founder Wendy Kopp has become a generational legend.[34]
- New Leaders for New Schools was founded by Jon Schnur, a Gen X staffer in the Clinton administration, with a mission to bring professionals with valuable and relevant experience in other management arenas into education.[35]
- The New Teacher Project (NTP), led by X'er Michelle Rhee, a TFA alumna, targets successful midcareer professionals to inject the same type of selectivity and performance into midcareer converts to the teaching profession that New Leaders does for school principals.[36]

Nonprofits and Social Entrepreneurship

Traditional nonprofits are increasingly applying top-quality business and management skills to the task at hand. Social entrepreneurship brings innovative, capitalistic business models to the service of social needs. The challenge for both types of organizations is to create extraordinary value with limited resources.

Your voices

I'm getting ready to job-swap with my wife, who will start working full-time for the first time since our early twenties. I'll be in a seminary/graduate school dual-degree program for the next four to five years, at which point I'd like to start a consulting firm to work with churches, ecumenical organizations, and maybe even secular organizations on conflict management and resolution. It's a drastic U-turn from the career that I was just starting to be really successful in, but I plan to fully leverage the lessons and experience I gained in the corporate world in this new, hopefully more fulfilling, venture.

The Trades and Other "Middle-Skill" Jobs

A significant number of jobs requiring medium levels of educational training—perhaps a two-year associate degree—still exist. True, these jobs are becoming a slightly smaller proportion of total employment, falling over the past two decades from 55 percent of all jobs in the United States to 48 percent. Nonetheless, they represent *almost half* of all employment opportunities today.[37] Some of the fast-growing jobs in this category include computer support specialists, carpenters, electricians, plumbers, dental hygienists, laboratory technicians, mechanics, truck drivers, chefs, and paralegals. Many of these jobs have experienced significant wage increases, based on tightening supply relative to demand, and are among the least likely to be subject to global labor competition since many of them have to be done locally. Many offer great opportunities for those of you who value independence and flexibility or who really prefer work that creates something tangible.

Your voices

I, too, was fed up with corporate life. I took a union job building elevators and have experienced not only job satisfaction, but reduced stress,

better pay, and less worry about appeasing those higher-ups who have no idea what is going on in their company. I couldn't have made a better decision five years ago. Not to mention that I have a pension, 401(k), and four weeks off a year that can be taken when I want to take it.

Most of us, the survivors anyway, have . . . a sense that the only way we'll get a fair shake is in a meritocracy, which is the furthest thing from a corporation you can get. This is why many of us went into cooking, IT, or some similar field . . . If you can cook or code, you can demand things.[38]

Government Service and the Military

Sixty percent of the federal government's General Schedule (rank-and-file) employees and 90 percent of the Senior Executive Service (federal government's top managers) will be eligible to retire in the next ten years. Because of the pensions available, these individuals almost certainly *will* retire.[39] The looming retirements mean that numerous openings are becoming available. Careers in government service offer the potential for both immediate impact and long-term security. The downside is limited financial upside.

Your voices

I am now thirty-five. I worked in corporate America, and now I work for government. That is an option worth considering . . . I have job stability; my government 401(k) type account is now over $45 thousand in value; I have full medical and three weeks' vacation per year that I do get to take; and I have a sense of mission that is motivated less by money than service. You have to like that idea because you won't get rich working for government, but you will get stability. And slow and steady wins the race. Government is going to need all the Gen X'ers it can get, and we are perfectly suited to government jobs.

You guys should have joined the military. We don't have a generation X vs. Y struggle. Plus, we get a pension at twenty years, job security, annual bonuses, and regular promotions. At forty-three, I'll retire with $70,000 per year for the rest of my life.

Bottom line on future jobs: Of course, you need to look for challenges that you personally find intriguing, ones that draw you in and areas that require innovation. Whatever you do, operate under the assumption that everything you know and do today will soon become a commodity. You may not want to climb the corporate ladder, but make pushing up the *knowledge* ladder an overriding priority.

In *The World Is Flat,* Thomas Friedman tells the story of his childhood friend Bill Greer, a freelance artist and graphic designer who worked with clients such as the *New York Times* in pretty much the same way for twenty years. For all those years, Greer produced camera-ready art, physical pieces that would then be photographed and prepared for publication. But beginning in about 2000, his world began to shift. Aided by sophisticated software, graphic design became a commodity. All of a sudden, anyone could produce an acceptable-quality product.

Greer pushed himself up the knowledge ladder, looking for work that his experience and talent would allow him to do, that young artists couldn't do equally well with technology for half the price. He moved into *ideation*—sketching creative concepts that then could be finished or illustrated by lower-paid individuals using computer programs.

The technology rapidly evolved yet further, and at the request of one of his clients, Greer used the latest technology to develop a specialization in *morphs*—a cartoon strip in which one character evolves into another. At the last telling, he was successfully working in this specialized area, but with one eye out for the next step up the ladder.[40]

In an edge economy, a key to maintaining career options is maintaining leading-edge skills.

CHAPTER SIX

Trading Up

Making the Organization You Work for Work for You

For most of you, work involves an organization. Although a small percentage of you are truly independent—say, artists or writers—for the vast majority of Generation X, success, no matter how you define it, requires navigating the complexities of an enterprise and balancing your preferences with the often-conflicting priorities of other people. Today almost 95 percent of you work within organizations that are owned or managed by others.[1] Most of the rest of you are independent contractors who work regularly with other businesses.

This chapter is about working more effectively with others, within an organization. It's about achieving success at this point in your career, on your terms, and by your definition—achieving what you want, now that you've evaluated your options and priorities.

True, Generation X measures success by many different criteria; the specific elements of your career plan need to be shaped to meet your own personal goals. But, to a large extent, getting *whatever* you want within an organization depends on your ability to be perceived as a valuable contributor. Working within an organization has parallels to sitting down at a poker table: your goal should be to acquire a large stack of chips because the chips, in turn, give you leverage. You can trade them in for whatever prize you most value. The fundamental rule of organizations is that you're unlikely to achieve any prize—more money, more control, more flexibility, anything—until you've accumulated a big pile of chips to trade.

Today, the challenge of gathering chips and of working effectively is complicated by a number of moving parts. Organizations are developing new ways of operating, establishing new rules, and creating different options and relationships. The ground under your feet is changing. And, in all likelihood, you're changing too. Being ten to twenty years into your career, where most Gen X'ers are today, raises three related issues:

1. *Shifting roles.* Over the course of a career, the roles you are expected to play shift. Some roles are primarily about content—producing whatever it is the business produces and "making the donuts." Your success depends on knowledge, technical or professional proficiency, and hard work. Other roles are responsible for managing processes, designing activities or overseeing people within the business. Most middle-management roles would fall in this category; success depends on your ability to organize and motivate. Many senior roles, in turn, are about context—that is, about establishing and reinforcing the values, strategies, policies, and leadership behaviors that set the stage broadly for the activities of the business; success depends on your ability to shape an environment in which other people succeed. The roles generally shift as you move higher in an organization from content to process to context. However, as traditional, hierarchical structures break down, the clarity of role progress is disappearing as well. Many senior roles today may have a significant content responsibility; traditional junior roles may have a larger influence on the

organizational context. Nonetheless, understanding your specific responsibilities in terms of these roles and modifying your behavior appropriately are the keys to progressing in your career. For many of you, the greatest changes occur at this point in your life.

2. *Evolving sense of self.* In chapter 2, I discussed the challenge of grounding yourself among the intrinsic landmarks of adult life. Developmental psychologists think in terms of moving to the next stage of adult development. Others describe a process of growing maturity or enhancing emotional IQ. However it's characterized, many individuals experience a subtle shift in focus around the ages you're at now—from developing yourself to developing those around you, from gauging success as an individual to measuring success through and with others. For many, the need to be the center of attention, what might be called the *star performer syndrome*, dims or even fades entirely. This shift has major implications for the roles that you can fill successfully at work; it's often difficult to be effective in a context-based role if your emotional needs are to be an individual star. As your needs shift, your ability to fill roles that involve promoting the success of others grows.

3. *Calibration of career potential.* At some point, most of us begin to calibrate our career expectations with reality—with our fundamental capabilities, with the time and energy we want to invest in our work, and with the demands imposed by our lives outside work. This is not to say that you won't achieve more and climb higher, if that's what you want to do, or even expand into new areas. You have time to do all this and more. But at this point, you have a more realistic view of what's possible. You understand more about the likely returns, given your talents and your inclinations for work. Some of you may have been disillusioned and found that your original aspirations are just not feasible, whether because of a bad-luck layoff or because of a reassessment of who you are. For

> many, this is when you make peace with the life you're leading and find constructive alternative paths. It becomes less about climbing and more about optimizing.

This chapter is about your work in the midst of organizations that are evolving toward new ways of working and lives that are experiencing the three interrelated shifts. While some of you may be planning to move out entirely and try the entrepreneurial route, for the majority of you, what's next involves charting a path that meets your goals *within* an organization of some size. Whether you are aiming for upper levels of management or prefer a role that allows you more flexibility to balance work with other life priorities, success within the organization will be key to achieving your goals. Again, if the fundamental nature of your work doesn't reflect things you find alluring—if it offers you little possibility of *ever* enjoying your work—I strongly urge you to begin moving in another direction. As outlined in chapter 4, finding work that aligns with your life lures is an essential baseline for a rewarding career.

Even if you're doing work that is potentially engaging, there's nothing surprising about feeling a bit stuck or confused or simply wanting to do more. This chapter is about being more effective and more successful with work. It's about:

- *Maximizing your effectiveness*—Playing to your strengths, creating the context for success, influencing the organization, understanding your role, and keeping up
- *Leveraging what you do*—Managing up, taking the initiative, or job-hopping
- *Expanding your options for greater long-term career sustainability*—Education, breadth, networking, and a cushion that allows you to walk away
- *Balancing the demands of the organization with other priorities in your life*—Being smart and lazy, reviewing the situation and letting

yourself off the hook, maintaining freeboard, and demonstrating grace under pressure

Increase Your Effectiveness at Work

Think about a consumer product. Commercial success doesn't necessarily mean that the product has the most or even the best features. It means there is coherence among the clearly communicated value proposition, targeted audience, and availability. It probably reflects a thoughtful positioning among other options and continual investments to keep the product up to date.

Maximizing your success in the work world requires the same logic, applied to you as an individual. Developing an effective career requires managing yourself well as a "product"—understanding your capabilities, being clear about your promises, and leveraging your time and energy in areas where they will have the greatest potential value. To increase your effectiveness, you need to:

- Play to your strengths
- Create the context for your success
- Influence the organization
- Understand each role you play
- Keep up

It's essential to get a clear picture of your strengths, to use them in compelling ways, and to continue to refine them as you move forward.

Play to Your Strengths

Perhaps the single most important thing at this point in your career, particularly during a difficult economy, is to play to your strengths. Earlier in your career, it made sense to try a bit of everything and push yourself to improve in areas of weakness. While self-improvement always makes some sense, the optimum strategy now is to do a lot of what you do best. You owe yourself the returns that come from focusing your time and energy. Your thirties and early forties are a time for consolidating your efforts in the places of maximum advantage. Zero in on what you're really good at, and what you're not:

1. *Imagine yourself as a product. How would you describe your features?* What do you do best? Where and how do you contribute maximum value? What would your colleagues say if asked?

2. What are your brand's liabilities—those features that are weakest, the ones that, frankly, someone should look elsewhere for?

3. *Are your perceptions of your strengths and weaknesses accurate and complete?* Get a reality check. Some of you may be lucky enough to have personal coaching; if so, take full advantage of the process for honest feedback on your current performance. Coaches, because they are not colleagues or bosses, can tell you things more forcefully and directly than the established organization will. If you don't have a personal coach, find someone who is removed from your direct work environment and can offer an independent perspective.

4. *How do your characteristics compare with those of others?* Get some perspective on your personal strengths and, more importantly, on how they are positioned among the range of possibilities. There are many useful tools, most online, each providing a slightly different lens. The Myers-Briggs assessment, for example, helps you understand how you perceive information and come to conclusions or make decisions.[2] These differences, based on Jungian philosophy, correspond to individuals' interests, reactions, values, motivations, and skills. Another highly useful tool is the right-brain/left-brain assessment, based on research demonstrating the lateralization of

brain function, that is, that the two sides of the human brain work in two different ways.[3] The tool helps you understand whether you are stronger at tasks that are visual, intuitive, and simultaneous (right-brained) or at tasks that are verbal, analytical, and sequential (left-brained). StrengthsFinder, a tool developed by Gallup Inc., is designed to find the top five things you do well.[4] Understanding your patterns more clearly provides a better basis for pinpointing areas for future success.

5. *How can you stand out?* What is distinctive or unique about you? Bring your personality, including your Generation X strengths—your skill with technology and networking, your humor, your quest for innovation—into the workplace as a source of differentiation. In the early stages of a career, success often largely depends on fitting in, on conforming with and performing against existing standards. But at this point in your career, it becomes increasingly important to stand out by showcasing your unique features and developing a consistent, signature reputation that tells others what it is like to work with you.

6. *Are you effectively communicating your brand?* Once you have a clear picture of your strengths and attributes, communicate those strengths to others and become better known for those traits. Consider the following:

   - *To the extent possible, are you choosing opportunities that demonstrate your strengths?* Are you making your logic known to others? For example, say, "I'd like to volunteer to be the project manager for this, because organization and meeting deadlines are my strengths."

   - *Do some of your auxiliary activities reinforce your "brand"?* For example, if you're involved in your local community, do you choose ways that support your focus, perhaps by volunteering for the school building committee, if you're good at managing projects; or for the local arts organization's long-range strategy committee, if that's your strength. These activities give you both broader experience and conversational ways to reinforce your capabilities and interests.

- *Do you reinforce your unique attributes through language and "voice"?* Think about the characteristics of the image you're developing, and how you could use specific language or perspectives to reinforce that image with others. For example, a person who is developing a reputation for analytical insights might preface comments with, "Based on the facts I reviewed . . ." or "Digging deeper, my analysis revealed . . ." In contrast, if your reputation built around your skill in talent management and development, you might bring your assessment of the possible impact of a potential initiative on the individuals involved into the discussion.
- *Do your peers reinforce the messages you're trying to send?* It's completely appropriate to ask colleagues to reference your successes by sending a note about a particular accomplishment to a broader group (and you should make a point of doing the same for them).

7. *What should you stop doing?* Eliminate things that are not your strong suit, whenever possible. Rather than taking on tasks that you're not good at, try to work closely with colleagues whose strengths complement yours.
8. *What should you teach others?* Attract people who want to learn what you do well by offering to share your expertise. Become known as the "go to" person in that area.
9. *Use your "brand" as a filter.* As you think about making additional career investments—for example, in education or in time devoted to the job—fine-tune your choices by considering the extent to which they support the strengths you're building.

10. Are you able to receive ongoing feedback? Have your coach or mentor, if you have one, give you feedback. Or find other ways to receive frequent input. Technology-based options are available, such as the innovative service Rypple, which supports anonymous, immediate feedback based on questions you pose to your selected panel of friends and colleagues.[5]

The key at this point is to build your work around things you do well and enjoy. Optimize. Focus on your strengths and use your best capabilities to greatest advantage.

Your voices

I struggled with finding satisfaction and happiness in the workplace for fifteen years. At one point I left to open a coffee shop. . . . I've moved jobs three times. I'm currently with an employer that I believe has got most of it right. The first thing I was asked to do was to complete my StrengthsFinder. After that, my goals were aligned with my strengths and opportunities identified to reach those goals . . . I feel a sense of relief in finding an organization that is trying and takes action to show that its employees are valued.

Create the Context for Your Success

Develop strong relationships with the people you need to do your work well. Create an organizational environment in which you will succeed. Research shows that working successfully with others depends highly on *trust-based* relationships. So it pays to make a significant investment in relationship building with the people with whom you collaborate or will need to collaborate to do your work. Being effective requires making positive *personal* connections with coworkers. People have to know each other well enough to recognize common values and goals before they're likely to share what they know, bring new insights into the discussion, and reach across organizational boundaries. Here are some steps:

1. Create a personal relationship map. Identify all the people who may influence the success of your work, everyone you need to collaborate with in order to do your job successfully. Ask yourself which ones you know well as individuals and which you need to know better.

2. Invest time and effort to form stronger relationships with each person. Start by leveraging tools and work activities that are already in place within your organization.

   - *Throughout the ongoing work process*—Take time from your normal work activities for personal interactions. Make a goal to become better acquainted with people as part of each process.
   - *Team and coworker selection*—Work with someone new. One rule of thumb: about three-quarters of the people on any assignment should be those you already trust to ensure the job is done well. But reach out to others about a quarter of the time for an influx of new ideas and continue to broaden your network.
   - *Technology*—Encourage your colleagues to use your firm's social networking tools not only for work-related exchanges, but also for sharing photos and news about personal events. Help colleagues who are not accustomed to social networking get started.
   - *Work location*—If possible, rotate your seating frequently, moving to different areas so that you are located near a variety of colleagues over time.
   - *Forums*—Take advantage of any activity that brings people together—social gatherings, customer-oriented events, special interest groups, educational programs, or any other forums your company offers—to get acquainted with new individuals.

3. If there are people who are key to the success of your work whom you don't get to know through any of these approaches, adopt a direct approach—seek them out and spend time with them. The key is being active in forming the strong personal relationships required to work effectively.

Influence the Organization

Success in business is *not* about having the most brilliant answer. It's about making things happen, and that means developing a really good understanding of the organization you want to have an impact on and the people you're trying to convince. So:

1. Understand your organization's written and unwritten rules. Each one has ways of operating that are not immediately apparent—codes that taken together represent a "hidden logic."[6] Listen to the advice colleagues share. Pay attention to their exact language. Understand the following:

    - Personal motivations—What is really important to people in this organization? What are your colleagues most excited about achieving?
    - Social enablers—Who is important and influential in this organization? Whom do others listen to?
    - Structural factors—How and when do key things happen?

2. Characterize your organization's hidden logic and consider where it is likely to thwart or support what you're trying to achieve.

3. Create the change you desire by influencing each element of resistance or support in multiple ways.[7] Create the motivation for change by answering "Should I change?" and "Will it be worth it?" at each of the following levels:

    - Personal motivation—Discuss core values and intrinsic satisfaction.

- Social motivation—Create peer pressure.
- Structural motivation—Align rewards and consequences.

4. Build the capability for change by answering "Can I do it?" and "Can I change?" at each of the following levels:

    - Personal capability—Build skills.
    - Social capability—Encourage collaboration and teamwork.
    - Structural capability—Put in place appropriate processes, systems, and data flow.

Understand Each Role You Play

Many midcareer problems stem from confusion around the nature of the role you're asked to play as you move through the organization. Here's an example. Alan was promoted from designer to first-line manager of the design team. He developed the very effective management approach of spending a few minutes every day with each team member, offering ideas and suggestions designed to push and challenge each designer's thinking. His group became known for high-quality work, and he was soon promoted to the next level in the organization, now managing the entire design department.

Alan continued with the management approach that had already proven highly successful, spending a few minutes with each designer, offering ideas and suggestions. Soon the entire department was in chaos. Projects were running late; designers were demoralized; teams were frustrated when pieces didn't come together as originally planned. What was happening?

Alan's role had shifted, but he hadn't adapted his management approach to reflect the shift. His first management role was essentially about making the content better, and the style he used worked well. His second role was not about content at all; it should have focused on the processes that tied the department together and the context for creating a stimulating environment. When he continued to focus on content, Alan was doing two things. He was not paying enough attention to the elements of his new role. Even more important, his increased positional authority meant that his ideas were no longer interpreted by the designers as suggestions intended to stimulate thinking. They now came across like orders, causing the designer involved to feel required to change course, even at the expense of project plans and schedules.

Here's another example. Based on some terrific, individual work, Barbara was viewed as a rising star and promoted at a young age to a senior position that involved managing many others, all of whom either were already acknowledged stars or were eager to become recognized. Success in this new role required creating a context in which all these individuals could be successful. It also meant nurturing them by promoting their accomplishments and acknowledging their needs for recognition. Barbara's work role had abruptly shifted from being about content, with success measured by standing out as an individual, to creating context. If continued, the very behavior that had led her to this point—her own personal achievements and "stardom"— would seriously interfere with her ability to execute the new role successfully.

Both these examples show how important it is that you understand the nature of your role and how it fits with your own preferred style and stage of development. And while your overall assignment may center around one set of activities, you are likely to encounter periodic events that thrust you into another role for a short time. These are often some of the most challenging sessions and the biggest opportunities to shine or fail spectacularly. For example, if you'll be attending a senior meeting for the first time, consider in advance this group's role in the organization to gain important clues about the nature of the discussion and the types of comments or contributions you could make. If you arrive without awareness of issues that are in the group's scope, at a minimum you are unlikely to make a useful contribution, and at worst, you may come across as annoying or irrelevant. Meetings are a bit of theater. Understand what role you are on stage to play.

A special note if you are taking on responsibilities as a member of a board of directors: governance roles, such those held by directors, ensure that the firm's activities are carried out according to acceptable standards. A board is responsible for ensuring that the right things are done; it is not responsible for doing them itself. In other words, your role as a member of the board is not to create context for the company; it is to assure yourself, to your full satisfaction, that the company is led by a management team that is both capable and fully motivated to create a successful context—including considerations of strategy, ethics, organizational development, and financial sustainability.

Keep Up

We live in an overwhelming world. You're dealing with information coming from all directions. In most cases, you face workloads that can never be completely done. There's always more to learn, to do, and to read. And it's likely that more people want to spend time with you than is physically possible.

Some useful books on the importance of prioritization essentially suggest that you understand the relative importance and urgency of each task and choose accordingly, tackling the urgent and most important first.[8] This sounds great, until you try to do it and find that almost everything on your list is important in some way and urgent to someone. How often have you started the day, confident that no matter what you did or didn't do, someone would be upset that you hadn't gotten to the task that they cared most about?

The key *is* to prioritize, but by using the three elements discussed above—your brand, your organization's hidden logic, and your specific role—to create a framework for determining what is important and urgent in your situation. Focus on activities that build your personal strengths, that set the stage for success within your organization, and that are congruent with your current role. Those should establish your priorities for what you do, what you learn, and the information you digest. The individual situations profiled in table 6-1 illustrate how these considerations may lead to distinct priorities.

TABLE 6-1

Prioritization for career success: What's really important and urgent for *you*?

If your brand is . . .	. . . and the hidden logic of your organization is . . .	. . . and the role you're currently in is . . .	Your priorities would likely be
Creative, out-of-the box thinker	Look out for yourself. Associate with important projects and people. Keep up the "right" image. Ignore administrative directives.	First-time project manager	Challenge is moving from individual star to leader of developing stars. Use your creativity to define intriguing goals for the project and attract the "best" individuals to your team based on your reputation. Learn how to help others develop their own creativity.
Empathetic, intuitive friend	Keep your head down. Don't rock the boat, criticize, or embarrass others. Fit in and develop strong social networks. Don't share negative results.	Individual contributor	Use your strong interpersonal skills to help the organization and increase your performance, perhaps by bringing new insights from one group to another. Make sure your empathy doesn't cause you to accept poor contributions or low standards in others.
Reliable, organized program manager	Gather no moss. Change jobs as quickly as possible. Keep your boss happy. Don't take on any project that might fail; keep your track record clean.	Senior leader	Challenge is moving from managing processes to creating context. Institutionalize your expertise in successful program management throughout the organization, through policies, normative practices, and sponsored education.
Charismatic client developer	Participate in the community. Share information. Respond to all requests for help quickly and enthusiastically. Bring something valuable to the table.	Team leader	Shift the empathy and enthusiasm you have exhibited with clients to develop insight into your team members. Help team members develop new approaches to distinctive response. Leverage your client relationships to bring new insights into the work of the team.

No one can be informed about everything that is happening in the world today, but through prioritization, you can keep up with what you need to be effective at work.

Leveraging Your Contributions for Success–By Any Measure

Assuming you're effectively performing your assigned role and contributing to the organization in ways that are generally viewed as valuable, you're in a position to leverage your accomplishments into success—*however you choose to define it*. You have accumulated a pile of chips and have the opportunity to cash them in.

Your voices

I have no trust (or even a modicum of respect) for the corporate model. I have been laid off, "repositioned," and downsized on multiple occasions, and each time none of those actions were performance related. Simply stated–it is difficult for me to demonstrate a great commitment and loyalty to an organization, knowing it really has no interest in my well-being.

Realistically, an organization is not a benevolent being. But that doesn't mean that the corporation doesn't have some wonderful assets. In general, you should assume that the corporate model fully encourages you to leverage these assets for your own benefit, based on the well-founded belief that what is good for you is also good for the corporation. Look at the corporation as a candy store, filled with great treats. Take full advantage of all it has to offer. Work the organization.

Your voices

Corporate life is great if you know how to work the system, something they don't teach you in a top-tier MBA program. If you're going to work for a large corporation with the mind-set that you will have an individual presence, you'll be unhappy from the start. I use corporations to meet my life objectives. I used one to obtain my MBA and CFA; they paid for everything. Then I left and found a job paying three times as much . . . I'm thirty-two and I will be able to retire in three years with over $5 million, at which point I'll be moving out of the country and essentially off the map.

Okay, that might be a bit extreme, but the ability of large organizations to provide you with rich benefits, broadly defined, is enormous if you take full advantage of the system. The candy of corporations is likely to include:

- *Training of all types*—Classes either within the company or externally on topics related to your job or, more broadly, languages, interpersonal skills, leadership, in-depth professional skills, or brief introductions to new areas that expand your perspectives and trigger your interest in learning more.[9]
- *Jobs you've never done but need to learn*—Lateral to your current position, but building your skill set, those capabilities you'll need in order to meet longer-term goals, like starting your own business in the future.
- *A fresh assignment*—Perhaps one that mixes roughly equal parts old and new responsibilities, perhaps in a different location or part of the organization lets you apply some of your existing skills, experience, and organizational contacts, while developing new ones. A relatively low-risk opportunity to try something fundamentally new.[10]

- *People you can learn from*—Smart people who know a lot about many different types of things (career tips or something useful completely outside the corporate world); diverse people (young, old, different races and backgrounds).[11]

- *Travel opportunities*—Often places to which you wouldn't likely travel on your own.

- *Funding for investments*—What better way to try a new venture idea out than to get funding from the corporation?

- *Robust processes and methodologies*—Essential skills for senior business leaders, like rigorous financial and risk analysis.

- *Benefits that cover your family*—One spouse can experiment with an entrepreneurial activity, while the other maintains the corporate benefits for the family.

- *Support for causes you care about*—Often in the form of monetary contributions from the corporation or time off to spend on community activities.

- *A chance to get away*—A sabbatical, if available, one of the best ways to rejuvenate, personally and professionally, from the routine of the job.[12]

Whatever appeals most to you, there are three basic strategies for using your track record of accomplishment and contribution to attain the types of rewards you value and cash in:

1. *Managing up*—An essential strategy in almost every circumstance

2. *Taking the initiative*—An option if you who want something different within your current organization

3. *Job-hopping*—An option if you who are particularly interested in moving up the hierarchy and/or increasing your compensation

Managing Up

Managing up is about working through the organization's channels to obtain more of whatever you use to gauge success: more money, control, autonomy, flexibility, learning, challenge—whatever. For many of you, this means working through Boomers who hold more senior positions. Don't assume that Boomers will automatically have insight into your priorities. Relationships between X'ers and Boomer bosses are often complicated for both parties. You've proven to be a challenging group for Boomers to manage, in part because a lot of them just don't get you and in part because you really don't care to be managed. As a group, midcareer employees today (that's you) have the lowest satisfaction rates with their immediate managers and the least confidence in top executives. Only one in three agree that top management displays integrity or commitment to employee development, and one in four say that they often disagree with the organization's policies on important employee matters.[13]

Your different approaches to work have confused Boomers. According to Lynne Lancaster and David Stillman, "When X'ers entered the workforce, most of us assumed they'd view the world of work the same way the Boomers had and that our tried-and-true management methods would work just fine. That turned out to be painfully wrong. Generation X'ers behaved differently from their predecessors and the organizations that didn't take the time to get to know them are still paying the price in high turnover, low hiring rates, and poor morale.[14]

One of Boomers' biggest worries is that you disengage too easily when the workday is done. You don't exhibit the same emotional ties to the corporation that they have come to value. As William Strauss and Neil Howe wrote in *The Fourth Turning,* "The perceived problem won't be whether 13ers [X'ers] work enough, which they will, but rather their distance from corporate culture. They will follow the contract—when it's time to work, they will focus, but when it's quitting time, they will disengage."[15] Boomers don't understand this approach; they want to know that you "care."

And, ironically, despite their own anti-authoritarian sentiments, Boomers are often surprised that you don't want to be managed. They often don't recognize Gen X's high need for individual responsibility, not realizing that many of you made major decisions at an early age, a childhood experience far removed from their own. According to author Michel Muetzel, "In the past, managers built responsibilities from ground zero . . . Business managers were molded through a basic apprentice structure, given small bits of responsibility at a time. These new young managers have been managing responsibility since they were eight years old. They had more responsibility for their own safety, their own time, at age eight than you and I did when we were almost twice that age."[16]

Boomers also often fail to recognize the value you place on having ownership in the process, involvement in the design, and access to transparent information. Throughout childhood, many X'ers were not only empowered but were often primary decision makers in their own lives.[17] Inclusiveness in decisions is paramount to X'ers. You crave being trusted. You don't like directive leadership styles and resent micromanagement, bosses who check on even the most trivial responsibilities. Unfortunately, these preferences are at odds with the way large corporations traditionally operate.

So it's not surprising if you find your Boomer boss doesn't quite think the way you do or anticipate what you want. To cash in your chips in the corporate world, you may need to take the initiative to bridge the gap with your Boomer managers. Unfortunately, many X'ers have *not* taken the initiative and have *not* stopped to push back or ask why. Rather than lobby effectively, X'ers often just go their own way, as they have been conditioned to do.[18]

Your voices

What we don't do well is sell ourselves and our work product (since we tend to assume our employers don't really care anyway). That's our fault.

Here are four steps to building more constructive relationships with your Boomer managers and managing up:

1. Understand how your boss is being measured and what he or she cares about. Identify specific things you can to do help your manager look and *be* more successful.

2. Clearly communicate exactly what you want (once you have a pile of chips, not before). Bosses are not mind readers; don't assume that they are unwilling to give you what you want if you haven't made your preferences explicit. And don't walk out the door without communicating first. That's a bad X'er habit.

3. Communicate successes, your own and those of others, fairly and regularly. Most X'ers don't do this enough. It's not sucking up; it's expected corporate behavior.

4. Make giving you what you want easy for your boss. The "brand" reputation you've built should be consistent with the reward you want (dependable delivery, if you want more flexibility; creative ideas, if you want more challenging projects).

Of course, not every reporting relationship involves an older Boomer. In some cases, you may be reporting to another X'er or even have a much younger boss. Here are two tips:

1. Go out of your way to signal that you respect the talent and skill of the other person. A patronizing attitude is annoying and destructive. Even if you may have more experience than your boss, the boss may have some valuable new perspectives.

2. Figure out how your boss likes to communicate and do your best to adapt. In general, the younger the employee, the more frequently he or she is accustomed to interacting. Don't interpret frequent messages from a younger boss as a lack of trust, but rather as a difference in communication style and habit.

Taking the Initiative

While I loved many things about the company I worked for out of graduate school, there were many times when I felt frustrated. As at most big companies, a number of processes seemed hopelessly bureaucratic and ripe opportunities appeared to go begging. Why on earth didn't someone deal with that? One day, the obvious realization sank in: *I* could deal with it myself.

Whenever you hear yourself thinking, "Why doesn't *someone*. . . ?" consider whether you might just do it yourself. If the opportunity you want doesn't currently exist, take the initiative to create it. Take responsibility for making your firm a better place for yourself and your colleagues, a more engaging work environment. Offer constructive suggestions *and* express willingness to do the work required to put new programs in place. Step into a leadership vacuum.

Map out how to make your idea happen. Take the lead in convincing others, using the six influence factors discussed earlier. Here are some ideas to consider:

- Change the rules of your job by plotting your next move up the value chain (not necessarily up the hierarchy). Take your normal task one step beyond in terms of value added. Add an analysis and recommendation to your original work. Over time, delegate your original task to someone else. Make yourself obsolete in your current role.

- Change the rules of your department or group by becoming what we call a *boundary spanner*, someone who interacts effectively with other groups inside or outside the firm and shares knowledge and insights in ways that bring new thinking and perspectives.

- Change the rules of business by operating in your sphere of responsibility according to the principles of the new economy. Being open, sharing, and acting globally are the goals; specific tactics to achieve them include creating an infrastructure for collaboration, getting the structures and governance right, making sure all participants can harvest some value, and abiding by community norms.

Your voices

As a younger Gen X'er, I don't understand why everyone doesn't take more control over their own corporate destiny. There are companies out there (large and small) that give you the ability to make an impact on a corporate level. You just have to find the right company and the right niche within the company . . . I strongly believe in the principle of "innovation without permission" . . . Who knows, you might even find ways to be more productive, bring in more revenue, and make work a much more enjoyable place.

There's one very important corollary to the lesson of taking initiative: first, do what you've committed to do—well. Never assume that taking on a new project, even one that is widely viewed as useful and important, excuses falling short on your original objectives. If taking on the new initiative will prevent you from completing your current assignment well, you will first need to renegotiate your objectives.

Job-Hopping

Job-hopping has been a classic X'er approach to increasing your level of organizational responsibility and/or compensation, often with significant success.

Your voices

I didn't get off to a slow start. My career started in 1993 and I hopped from job to job, each with a great raise.

Whether driven by opportunities for advancement, layoffs, shifting interests, or geographic preferences, most of you have changed jobs multiple times in your careers thus far. Americans change jobs an average of eleven times during their lives, and much of that statistic is driven by the restlessness of Gen X.[19]

Strauss and Howe wrote of X'ers, "what the *Wall Street Journal* calls 'high-tech nomads' will be the fungible workers of the . . . globalized economy. They will barnstorm the marketplace, exploring its every cranny, seeking every edge, exploiting every point of advantage. They will talk about jobs rather than careers, what they can get done by the end of the day. Their low-sweat, task-efficient work style will be good for the U.S. profitability."[20]

Your voices

Beth Hilbing, currently forty-four, is a highly respected CIO for a division at Northrop Grumman. In addition to her direct responsibilities, Beth is active in various cross-company activities, including college recruiting and Habitat for Humanity, and serves on a number of non-profit boards.

Since I was twelve, I've worked in department stores, banks. Right after high school, I took a full-time job and went to college part-time.

I never pinpointed a certain field. I knew I was really good at creating things from scratch, that I get a lot of pleasure out of completing difficult tasks. I have a strong desire to do things that create change. I like to have an impact on colleagues and customers. And I have a very high work ethic. I've been open to what came my way.

I got into IT a bit haphazardly. There was an opening and the opportunity for increasing responsibility. I got my first management role at twenty-six.

Since then I've worked for seven companies over twenty-four years. A couple of the moves were relocations based on my husband's

career, but most were driven by feeling that I'd exhausted the available options or that it would take too long to get ahead where I was employed. Basically I've moved for career elevation. I've never had any difficulty moving or changing directions.[21]

Job-hopping makes sense if the currency you most want to receive when you cash in your chips is not available at your current firm. For most, that means access to more money, more authority, or different learning opportunities, although in truth any currency could serve as the motivation to job-hop.

If you do job-hop as a way to leverage your accomplishments, pay special attention to how you come and go. The first and last weeks are critically important. You are in a strong spotlight. You have great opportunity for upside when you arrive and tremendous potential for downside when you leave. You shape your reputation, for good or bad in the way you come and go.

I once hired someone to help me dig out of my work overload. The new guy stopped by my office right after signing all the requisite forms. "What are your top three issues?" he asked. Hmmm. A bit of an odd start, but okay, I'll play along. I shared my top three headaches, all complicated issues with multiple constituencies and intricate ramifications to sort out. As I spoke, he made a few scratchy notes on a little pad. When I finished, he didn't comment or ask a single question, just nodded and backed out the door, leaving me very disappointed and feeling that I'd just added a fourth major headache to my list. To my amazement, he reappeared in my doorway at the end of the day. "Done," he said. "What are the next three?"

Now I wouldn't exactly recommend that as the perfect way to start a new job. At a minimum, it stressed the new boss. But I would say that in terms of making an impression—not just a good impression, but one that will last for decades—this guy was *the* master. Bar none, the best I've ever seen. In contrast, I've seen many begin employment in ways that made little impression at all or, worse yet, that made everyone wonder who hired this guy anyway.

Of course, some people leave better than others. Those who do it well go out of their way to touch base with colleagues to ensure that they have everything they need going forward. Those who do it well make you feel that even though they are leaving, they wish you and the company success.

The fundamental philosophy of job-hopping is that both leaving and joining are times when your primary focus must be (or must appear to be) firmly fixed on the company and your colleagues. Both are times when the questions, "What do you need?" and "How can I help?" should be heard most clearly. Neither are times when you talk about yourself and what you want, but are times to give back. You'll be repaid repeatedly in terms of the reputation you build.

Expanding Your Options

When I listen to X'ers describe their career strategies, I often feel that I'm watching a soccer goalie in the net, someone warily watching the opposing team, getting ready to dart to the right or the left, depending on the direction the ball takes. Most of you tell me about the options you've thought through: your current focus, the seeds you're planting for a second career, and the ways you'd approach a third or fourth should the need arise. Your description almost always includes the phrase "*if* something bad were to happen." While currently you may be working hard for one company, most of you are also thinking about alternatives and possible future moves. For X'ers, security and self-reliance come from expanding your options. You've already identified, and as generation excel at, three key strategies for keeping your options open.

1. Education

2. Breadth

3. Networking

Education

From the beginning, education has been a key part of your game plan. You are already well educated and continue to study. X'ers are, in fact, better educated for your age than any other generation. Thirty-one percent of you have college degrees.[22] Nearly one in ten holds a graduate degree.[23] About 6 percent of you are still enrolled in school, many in pursuit of an advanced degree. Many of you participate in work-related courses or less formal work-related learning activities, such as seminars offered by employers.[24] For your generation as a whole, your education has paid off; your income is directly related to your educational achievement. Those of you with advanced degrees substantially outearn others.[25]

For those of you with the option of continuing education, two disciplines are particularly important today:

1. *Finance, including a sophisticated understanding of return-on-investment analysis.* Regardless of your role, it is essential to have a high level of comfort with financial concepts. As organizations develop new business models to create value, personally understanding the embedded economics and trade-offs involved is essential. You must be able to interpret the financial reports for your business, understand the key points of leverage, and comfortably use return-on-investment concepts, including net present value and the internal rate of return, to discuss options.

2. *Marketing and branding savvy.* The classic concepts of marketing—the connections between all the elements of the offering, as well as world-class skills in survey research, segmentation, targeting, positioning, and communication—are important to master. Again, you need this regardless of your specific role. The increased ease of communication means that multiple people represent your brand in thousands of daily interactions with customers, suppliers, and each other. While the *communication* of traditional brand shorthand—logos and slogans—is yielding diminishing returns, the *existence* of a cohesive "brand" experience is growing in importance.

Breadth

Many X'ers hate to put too many eggs in the corporate basket. You don't like feeling boxed in, having your freedom or options reduced. You don't like to be pigeonholed or pushed out on a limb of specialization, with the inherent danger of a whimsical corporation sawing that limb off during the next restructuring.

Of course, in most traditional corporate career paths, boxing people in, by urging them to specialize or to take on managerial roles that remove them from the skill of the business, is exactly what organizations do to people in their thirties and forties. Most corporate career paths narrow at the top; the perceived range of options diminishes as individuals become increasingly identified with specific functions or roles. The sense of narrowing career paths and increased vulnerability is often most palpable at the transition from middle to upper management, just where many of you are today.

Your voices

I completely agree about not wanting to climb too high . . . if I take a step up, I become specialized and if that string gets cut, I'll be out of work. So I sit at my current position getting by, when I should have been able to buy a house of my own by now. Don't get me wrong, I have the initiative and drive to improve and grow and have improved my field beyond anyone's hopes, but a move up the corporate ladder feels like a loss . . . there's no falling back to where I am now if I go that way.

To keep your options open, many of you have chosen one of two basic strategies: avoiding specialization or systematically adding more areas of specialization to your repertoire. Avoiding specialization may provide a fungible set of skills, but may not offer the financial upside that would be available with greater focus.

Your voices

Rory Madden, thirty-nine, is an executive with a major oil company. Born in Scotland, he has a degree in mechanical engineering from the University of Edinburgh and lived and worked in London before moving to Houston four years ago. Never married, Rory has a close circle of friends, including five or six from his boarding school days.

I've always taken the contrary view. Everyone was going to be an accountant or banker. I decided I would go in another direction. The contrary view leads to less competition. Why run with the herd when I don't have to? I chose mechanical engineering because it provided a base level of education. It kept most of my options open in terms in career choice.

But I made the decision early in my career that there was no technical road to success. I thought if you understood the people process, then you'd have great transferable skills. If the company went bankrupt, if the industry was down, I could always jump ship. My industry pushes you very hard up a technical ladder. I rebelled and went for a commercial role. I didn't want to be a functional expert.

There are pros and cons from this decision. I have more options, but it was a bad financial decision in today's market. There is a lot of money to be made as a technical expert. The way I've gone, haphazard, every day I have to sing for my supper. But I have transferable skills. I'm a jack-of-all-trades guy. I don't feel vulnerable from a skills-set perspective.[26]

The alternative way of creating breadth is to master a number of different specialties.

Your voices

Eric Kimble is forty-one-years old and married with three children. He graduated from Harvard Business School in 1994 and is currently *successfully employed as a senior marketing and sales executive at Cubist, a $400 million, rapidly growing, biopharmaceutical firm.*

My career strategy has been to build a broad foundation. I didn't just want to move up within one function, like Jack climbing the beanstalk—thin at the top and easy to fall over. My goal has always been to build a wide base. I started in market research, moved to field sales, went back to manage people in marketing research, and then moved into marketing. I then felt my beanstalk was getting a little thin, a little ungainly, so I asked to be in sales. That was considered a little unusual—to move to sales after building a strong marketing career—but I saw it as a step sideways to make my career strong. Today I'm the head of sales and have a broad background to do the job well. As I made these moves, I went from a company with fifty thousand employees, to one with three thousand, to now, four hundred.

I think of myself as generally risk averse. I take only very, very calculated risks. Measured. Thoughtful and careful. On paper, some of my career moves might have looked rash, like taking a jump to sales, but the whole time I was in marketing, I was gauging what was happening in sales. I'm now thinking that if I want to be in general management, I might have to go into manufacturing for some time.

My bottom-line strategy is to become excellent at a few things at a time. Being excellent gives you inner strength. If you tackle too many things too quickly—if you're mediocre at a dozen things—you'll never excel.[27]

And, as always, there are those who disagree.

Your voices

Create an individual contributor career path: the technical architect, the finance specialist, the special projects researcher, the marketing strategist . . . Many of us want to lead by example, to be the go-to fixer, to spearhead projects.

Networking

One of Generation X's strongest characteristics—and best source of future options—is the network of friends you've formed and maintained. Network theorists describe two broad categories of relationships: *strong ties*, or relationships that go back years and are based on trust and reciprocity, and *weak ties*, those acquaintances with whom we do not have a strong emotional attachment and in fact, at this moment, may not even know.[28] Lynda Gratton, a professor of management practice at the London Business School, notes, "The truth is that new ideas and insights usually come not from strong ties but rather from the many weak ties that people have."[29]

Ethan Watters, in his exploration of Generation X's urban tribes, noted that your tribe gives you access to many individuals outside the apparent boundaries of the group. Individual members have other connections that extend outside—to people they've met at other times or know from other aspects of their lives. Through them, you are—even if you don't know it—connected to a broad network of contacts and resources or weak ties.[30]

The benefits of being part of this broader community are substantial, often leading to a mushrooming of possibilities in your career and other aspects of life.[31] As Watters found,

> *My tribe provided me with two seemingly contradictory benefits simultaneously. It offered me emotional shelter by giving me a half-dozen strong ties clustered together, while at the same time connecting me to the city with hundreds (possibly thousands) of weak ties that ran from friend to friend and tribe to tribe.*[32] *. . . [Putnam, in his book* Bowling Alone*] dropped the ball when it came to understanding the social dark matter hidden in our weak ties . . . my network of weak ties made me feel uniquely connected to the swirl of city life in our modern times.*[33]

Your voices

Mike Dover, born in 1968, is a successful Canadian professional and colleague at nGenera. Mike, who is married, graduated from college in 1991.

I'm a super social networker.

I'm in touch with all my old bosses. I ask candidates to tell me about their favorite boss and what they learned from him or her. If the person has never had a favorite boss, I stop listening to them; they haven't taken advantage of the experiences they've had. I look for people who say that their favorite boss gave them a long leash, but also gave them an "Uncle Joe" talk when necessary and always had their back in public. That's the type of boss I value, and that I aspire to be.

I stay in contact with about one hundred fifty past clients. I could get you in touch with at least ninety by the end of the day.

My high school friends and I are still very close. The group gets together at least quarterly and always spends New Year's Eve together. Thirty-six of us went on a trip recently; two got married on the trip and two celebrated their fortieth birthdays. We're all going on another together soon.

Being active online is important. I have 451 people in my LinkedIn network. I wouldn't interview a candidate who didn't show up on Google.

If massive layoffs were to occur at my company, I'd be fine. I'd make one hundred phone calls and say, "Hey, I'm available. I need help figuring out my next move. Hey, what's going on in your organization?" I have lots of options I'd be able to tap.[34]

Balancing the Needs of the Organization with "Life"

One of the biggest work challenges for many in Generation X is to balance the demands of the organization with those of "life." You put a lot of pressure on yourself to be excellent and to do it all. It's easy to get swept up into the never-ending demands of work.

Your voices

The truth is I don't want to go into management. I feel work-life balance is more important and realize managers don't last too long. They tend to burn out too fast. I would rather work in a lower-paying position and have security and free time.

There are ways to balance these conflicting demands—to excel at work and have a life. Here are three suggestions:

1. *Be smart* and *lazy*—Think outside the box and leverage new approaches.
2. *Follow Fagin's advice*—Review the situation and let yourself off the hook on some things.
3. *Maintain freeboard*—Build contingencies into your commitments.

Be Smart and Lazy

As the former head of Disney Imagineering, Bran Ferren, was giving a speech, he drew a two-by-two grid, with one axis labeled "smart" and "dumb" and the other, "energetic" and "lazy."[35] "Which of the four quadrants would you prefer your employees be in?" he asked. The audience pretty quickly agreed that "dumb and lazy" was bad, and "dumb and energetic" was probably even worse (imagine the damage they could do). But there was disagreement on the two "smart" options. Most people immediately gravitated toward "smart and energetic." Wouldn't that be great? Smart people running around like mad, doing all sorts of energetic things? Perhaps. But Ferren argued that the optimum choice would be "smart and lazy." Those are the people who are likely to step back and rethink whether there just might be an easier way. Take a practical and forward-thinking approach to figuring out how to get things done with the least possible fuss. Be smart—and lazy.

One of the great advantages today, of course, is technology. I know that BlackBerrys interrupt family time and encroach on your nights in this global economy, but it doesn't have to be that way. If you closely observe younger Y's (those born after 1983 or 1984, who were teens when social media like MySpace and Facebook were taking off), they are far less controlled by technology than many X'ers. They turn it off. And they respect each other's right to be offline for periods of time, probably because they are more accustomed than most of us to asynchronous communication. They post without expecting instant response.

Your voices

As an "older" Y, even I didn't quite understand what Facebook meant to my sister, a recent grad, and her friends, until I finally started using it semi-regularly. Understanding how Y's use sites like this—that they aren't just for e-mail or networking, but practically for conducting *life*—could go a long way to ease X'ers' technology anxiety.[36]

Using technology to make life simpler and to give you more freedom and flexibility is essential today. In chapter 8, I'll talk about establishing workplace norms that make it comfortable for everyone to establish boundaries around the times when they will not be available for work communication.

Meanwhile, many X'ers are guarding a closely held secret: you're not *all* as comfortable with the technology that is changing how things are done as everyone seems to think you are. True, you grew up playing *Pong*, but Web 2.0 technologies are evolving at an astonishing pace; new applications are becoming available in droves. While X'ers are perceived as very tech-savvy, some of you—not all, I know, I know—don't feel as comfortable with technology as the perception indicates. And while it's perfectly acceptable for Boomers to admit ignorance and ask for help, it's often embarrassing for X'ers to do so because of your reputation for technological sophistication.

Your voices

I consider myself kind of a technology Luddite. I struggle. I learned it late and have a hard time keeping up.[37]

As for the modern IT resources, yep, I must admit, I'm not up on most of them—and finding someone to teach you seems near impossible.

Technology, particularly social media, can help you work smart and lazy. Push yourself to experiment with and adopt new applications.

Follow Fagin's Advice

Sometimes things go crashingly wrong. Things happen, and it becomes obvious that what you expected to accomplish is no longer remotely possible.

In *Oliver Twist,* the character Fagin leads a gang of children who work the streets as pickpockets. Not the most inspirational figure, perhaps, but he has a habit that is most useful when it comes to balancing work pressures. When in the tightest spots, he steps back and thoughtfully considers his options. In the musical version, *Oliver!,* he sings: "I'm reviewing . . . the sit-u-a-tion . . . I think I'd better think it out again!"[38]

When all else fails, don't panic. Let go of the idea that you've got to make *this* work. Lay out the alternatives—even the most distasteful ones—and look for reasonable shortcuts and compromises. Negotiate a new path forward.

Mike, for example, was in a difficult spot. Despite working overtime for several weeks straight, the project he'd committed to deliver was woefully bogged down and behind schedule. His team was stressed and demoralized, and the deadline for delivery to the customer was looming. He took a deep breath and, first, acknowledged the reality of the situation to himself. Then he took a hard look at the options. He could:

- Call the customer and negotiate an extension of the delivery deadline, not great in terms of customer delight, but better than surprising it with bad news at the very last minute.

- Hire additional team members, perhaps contractors who could begin immediately; this would not be great for the budget but might help meet the deadline, assuming they could get up to speed quickly.
- Review the project specs; could the project be completed to the customer's satisfaction with fewer "bells and whistles"?
- Develop a compromise offer; perhaps by understanding the customer's needs more clearly, it would be possible to deliver an essential part of the promised deliverable on schedule and the remainder later.

The key point is to step back and lay out as many creative options as possible. And let yourself off the hook on some things.

Maintain Freeboard

Advice on relationships often focuses on negotiating agreements: committing to yourself and your significant other what you are and are *not* going to do; putting limits on your professional commitments; agreeing on your family responsibilities.

This advice is certainly a reasonable starting point, but from my experience, it's woefully inadequate. The key to being a good partner in any sphere—as a spouse, parent, or employee—is to be able to respond to situations that go beyond anything anticipated in the commitments. No matter how carefully you plan, unexpected things will happen. It's essential to maintain some *freeboard.* (Freeboard is a sailing term, referring to the amount your boat's side sticks out of the water. If you weigh your boat down too heavily, you won't have enough freeboard to withstand big waves when they crash over the bow.)

Ideally, arrange each dimension of your life to allow moment-to-moment flexibility. Part-time work on a rigid, fixed schedule is often more difficult than a full-time job that allows you to duck out for the afternoon for an emergency on the home front. Child care in an institution that charges outrageous fees for every minute you're late for pickup adds stress. Of course, you want to keep your commitments whenever possible, but the best arrangements are those that allow some moment-to-moment flexibility, the ones that recognize that stuff happens. So, for example, if you're coming back from maternity leave and would like to arrange a reduced work schedule, I recommend you propose a flexible schedule, rather than predetermined days per week. Even if you almost always work the same days each week, having the flexibility built into the arrangement will be better for the company and you. You give the company access to your skills as needed (for example, to come in on an unscheduled day to attend an important meeting). Of course, you'll need to arrange the same degree of flexibility in your child-care arrangements, but you'll have the ability to respond to both work and family emergencies.

In all likelihood, you have options available that you (and most of your colleagues) have not tapped. Most companies offer arrangements with wide variations in time and place: flexible time, including individualized work schedules, flexible shifts, and compressed workweeks; reduced time options, including a variety of part-time work, job sharing, and leaves of absence; and flexible place, including telecommuting (working primarily from home) and mobile work (such as a salesperson who works predominantly on the road). Some companies also offer sabbaticals and paid or unpaid leaves of absence. Some will structure a contract relationship. In many organizations, social norms inhibit employees from taking some of the options offered. It's time to move past and consider what would work for you and negotiate to get it.

In negotiating, the first conversations you need to have on these issues are with your direct boss. Go armed with a thoughtful, unemotional analysis of the pros and cons of the arrangements you'd like, translated into financial language, that is, return-on-investment terms. Include information on the ways you will mitigate any cons. Build in a contingency plan for addressing any unforeseen developments. Make your immediate supervisor comfortable with the proposal, gain his or her support, and then go through any policy-setting channels, such as human resources, to request official confirmation.

Ironically, the biggest trick to working successfully within an organization is to be grounded in terms of what you're good at and what you really want. When you've established your credentials and clarified your goals, the challenge is to communicate clearly and persuasively, while continuing to build both your personal capabilities and your back-up options.

CHAPTER SEVEN

Branching Out

Alternative Workplaces and Portfolio Careers

More than any other contemporary generation, you have been attracted to work that offers alternative arrangements and a portfolio of options. Working independently, founding entrepreneurial ventures, joining small firms, and juggling multiple jobs simultaneously are hallmarks of Generation X.

Your voices

My aversion to power structures and rules is deeply ingrained and made it hard to enter the corporate workforce in my early twenties. After a few professional near-catastrophes, I finally figured out how to posture myself in the workplace, feel content, and be successful. But lurking in the back of my mind and always at the fore of my daydreams is this, "How can I get out of here?"

On the surface, this appears to be another of your generation's conundrums. Just as you are simultaneously independent and group oriented, you value security yet often choose what others might view as risky paths toward this goal. Your teen years provide perspective on both riddles. The responsibility you bore as teens both increased your confidence in your ability to take care of yourself and drove you closer to your friends for support. You came to value both self-reliance and membership in a close-knit circle of friends—a tribe. Your desire for self-reliance, in turn, plays out in seemingly contradictory ways. For some of you, it means pushing to reach even higher levels in large organizations (while staying vigilant for ways to broaden your base and heighten your career sustainability). For others, however, this same desire for self-reliance is pushing you away from large organizations into a wide variety of alternative arrangements, small firms, entrepreneurial ventures, and, for an increasing number, a portfolio of multiple careers, work affiliations, and employment arrangements. Through it all, your friends and the families you are creating remain an important priority and, for most, an essential source of tangible, emotional, and intellectual support.

The common denominator for most X'ers is the desire for greater control over your own destiny. Your views on the best way to achieve a sense of control, however, differ substantially.

Your voices

It was abundantly obvious to me that there were shortcomings to being an employee in a large, established firm—in terms of your ability to control your time, impact, and destiny. It was fairly obvious what my career path would look like. There was little I could do to influence the timing or direction of that path. Entrepreneurial options allow you to control the environment and people with whom you work, to create your own culture and own norms.[1]

What works? Sticking to your job and becoming a true asset to the company, not just someone who shows up to get a paycheck. You really have to learn to love the plateau of working for a living at a corporation. Then you can appreciate the rewards that come from doing your job well—pay increases, job promotions, awards, building your wealth with your company match in a 401(k) retirement fund, and building lifelong friendships.[2]

This chapter is for those of you who, unlike this last voice, are drawn to being independent, entrepreneurial, or part of a small company. Probably the most universal desire of those of you who choose these alternatives over becoming an ingrained, established member of a large organization is to influence directly the decisions that govern your career and your life. Although most researchers agree that there is no neat set of behavioral attributes that describe an entrepreneurial personality, it does appear that entrepreneurs have a high desire to be in control of their own fate.

Your voices

While I'll never be eating steak and caviar every night, I won't starve and the bills will get paid. I'll never work for another large company ever again . . . I can see my kids any time I want, take a class if I want, take a day off when it's nice out. I have the ability to throttle forward or cut back on the amount of work I'm willing to do. Since we all have to work to earn a buck, it's better to have some control of the one thing you can't buy back: time.

Beyond control, X'ers' drive into alternative arrangements is motivated by a number of related considerations—a desire to express your creativity, the competing demands of your family commitments, concerns about the corporate path, and bottom-line necessity. For many of you, the desire to do it yourself is an important driver. There's also a loyalty to the independent sensibility that makes it hard to accept a materialist corporate culture. Add X'ers' deep mistrust of authority and the organization's commitment, and it's not surprising that so many of you are choosing to step away from the corporation.

Your voices

Seriously? Corporations need us? They treat us like commodities and are surprised when we become mercenaries. Given that there's no such thing as corporate loyalty, the logical thing for a Gen X'er to do is to start a company . . . I started my own company. It's small, but I won't be downsized, laid off, or outsourced. It pays very good retirement, because I'm in charge of the retirement plan.

Then there are the external realities. Layoffs have forced some of you to go on your own. Even if you are in the workplace, many of you feel crowded in corporate careers, concerned about a Boomer ceiling that will forever cap your upside potential. A number of you who left initially from necessity now find that it suits your needs better than the corporate role you were forced to leave.

Your voices

I've realized that there is no getting around the Boomer-clog on the upper end of the corporate ladder. These people are living longer and there's too many of them. So, rather than to contribute to their power base by working for them, I work for myself and contract with them. Heck, I employ them now. I'm taking what's mine because if I wait for the Boomers to give it to me, I'll never get it. In the meantime, I'll end up retiring before most of them, and that'll be the sweetest revenge of all.[3]

Of course, the full-on entrepreneurial route is not for everyone. It's not a consideration for many of you who prefer stability. Nonetheless, keeping your options open, diversifying your skills, and preparing for a work life that might not involve taking on that next corporate job is rarely far from most X'ers' mind.

This chapter discusses the realistic considerations of whether branching out—moving out of the large corporate environment or diversifying beyond one organization—is for you. It's about:

- The alternative workplace—Both small companies and independent arrangements
- The entrepreneurial route—Key lessons to minimize the risk
- Portfolio lives—Blending multiple careers as ways to spread the risk and lay the groundwork for future opportunities

The Alternative Workplace

Small companies and independent arrangements are a popular choice for X'ers who chose to leave the traditional corporate path. In a survey conducted in 2004 that was slightly skewed toward male and higher-income respondents, 38 percent of Gen X respondents said they worked for privately held companies or for a private individual.[4] Small-firm–based opportunities offer one way to reflect your X'er preference for a greater sense of control over your destiny and, as a result, more self-reliance. Moving down in company size often allows you to move up in responsibility and reward. It may give you a greater voice in the firm's destiny with regard to recruiting and people development, having your ideas heard, and planning strategy. The skills you've learned in a larger-company environment can really pay off.

Your voices

Size does matter . . . at least when it comes to companies. My last job was with a smaller company . . . I and other X'ers sped through the ranks with relative ease, thanks greatly to the professional experience gained in the last thirty-something years–the high work ethic, discipline and sacrifices we've learned to make.

And there's the material consideration. The small-company route often also brings the opportunity for equity involvement.

A second alternative, also popular with Generation X, perhaps because of your "outsider" self-identity, is to work on a contract basis, in what the Bureau of Labor Statistics calls alternative work arrangements. Compared with other generations, a slightly higher percentage of you are classified in this a category, which encompasses independent contractors (including most of those also classified as self-employed), on-call workers (such as substitute teachers), temporary agency workers, and people who work for contract firms (such as lawn or janitorial service companies). Of those between the ages of thirty-five and forty-four, 10.9 percent were classified as having alternative work arrangements in 2005, compared with an overall average of 10.7 percent.[5] You classify yourselves as self-employed professionals 25 percent more frequently than older counterparts.[6]

Like the small-company route, contracting appeals to the need for autonomy, flexibility, and freedom from corporation lockstep. Contracting can isolate you from a tribe of workplace peers, but surprisingly, contractors aren't always loners. Sometimes this route can offer the best of both worlds—the corporate environment without competition, politics, or fear of layoffs.

Your voices

I have been in . . . industry for twenty-plus years as a full-time employee. A year ago I decided to become a contractor . . . I feel less

"burdened" with the politics of the current employer. I gravitate to my temporary colleagues who display true interest in getting the job done and collaborating . . . As a contractor, my peers fear me less–I'm a temporary fixture–but if they like me, and there's work to be done, I could be around for awhile. That's acceptable to them, again because I'm a contractor. They know I really don't care to get too deep into the office politics, but I care about them while employed there. It's been quite a pleasant surprise. I should have probably contracted years ago.

If you're thinking of alternative work arrangements, note that contractor or consultant-type work arrangements bring their own challenges. Here's a simple checklist of practical considerations.

- *Balance marketing with delivery*—You always have to be looking for your next job, even if you're head down on delivery of the current assignment. Find practical ways to balance both, perhaps by putting aside a specific time each week devoted to marketing.
- *Maintain your edge*—Stay current. Make sure you have a way to access new ideas and approaches, perhaps by connecting with a professional community.
- *Maintain client contact between engagements*—Develop an approach for managing client relationships when you're not directly involved in work through professional newsletters or other approaches.
- *Create your support infrastructure*—Solo work requires finding solutions for dozens of activities—from phone messages to invoicing—that large organizations seamlessly handle. A number of virtual and office-based options are emerging to provide flexible support.

Technology makes meeting these challenges easier, but developing the discipline to keep all the balls in the air when you're a solo practitioner or small enterprise can be difficult. If you're planning to go this route, be sure to consider in advance how you will address each of these challenges.

The Entrepreneurial Path

For some of you, there's no part-way. You simply want to own and run your own company. You want the entrepreneurial route.

Your voices

From a career perspective, everyone dreams about becoming an entrepreneur. For some, it's a control issue, like those who also want to be tri-athletes. Some are making lifestyle choices around their kids. But deep down inside, almost all of us want to be entrepreneurs. My advice: don't wait too long.[7]

Many of you who *have* jumped out sound very happy with your decision.

Your voices

I have already made the jump to my own entrepreneurial life. I have been at it for almost five years now, and I can safely say that a team of wild horses could not drag me back into the corporate world. I love being independent, making up my own rules as I go, and the freedom to work on what I want when I want to do it. If others from my generation get a taste of the entrepreneur's life, they will leave in droves. Once the genie is out of the bottle, it isn't going back in.

Statistical research bears out what your voices have already said: individuals who are self-employed are considerably more satisfied with their jobs than are other workers. They're more satisfied with their salaries, the job security, chances for promotion, level of on-the-job stress, flexibility of hours, and proximity of work and home.[8]

Many of you are venturing out on your own. Today, four of five business start-ups are headed by X'er's. Increasingly, entrepreneurship is the course in highest demand in many MBA programs, as you take classes, strengthen your finances, and dream up new business concepts.

What Are the Odds?

The good news is that the chances of entrepreneurial success are improving. The changes in the nature of work I discussed in chapter 5—smaller, niche-focused firms, businesses built on offering greater personalization or individualization, and business models based on shared or collectively created information—are opening new doors. New technologies reduce the advantages of scale and costs of transactions, making it easier for small players to jump into the market. Smaller firms, specialized around core competencies, are expected to proliferate. We may, in fact, be entering a golden age for the small entrepreneur. Thomas W. Malone, a professor at the Massachusetts Institute of Technology, estimates that the Internet and powerful new off-the-shelf technologies have created an environment in which one of ten small businesses will succeed, a much higher proportion than in the past.[9]

Good news? Absolutely. But even if Malone's forecasts are correct, that still leaves a *90 percent* failure rate. Realistically, choosing the entrepreneurial route means choosing the chance for disappointment. These businesses can represent a great roller-coaster ride. You have to be prepared for the big ups and possibly gut-wrenching downs.

Your voices

Dead on. . . . We're thinking of quitting the corporate world . . . but are afraid of the costs and risks. Maybe the corporate world is an OK place, but I don't want to be like my dad who was never a boss and still has to work at seventy-two.

Even in a successful start-up, there are trade-offs to consider. In most instances, the entrepreneurial route will reduce your immediate compensation. And it is likely to require long hours, days, and weeks. Even a lack of support from your immediate family can be a problem.

Your voices

It's difficult for our parents' generation to understand why we would choose an entrepreneurial route. It's a challenge to convince them it's an acceptable path. With the entrepreneurial route, there's likely to be negative reinforcement around the choices you're making.[10]

To help mitigate the downside risk and create buy-in from key supporters, approach your entrepreneurial venture with sound forethought. There are four things that you should nail down before you cut the cord.

1. A good idea
2. A good plan
3. Tangible resources—the right skills and enough money
4. Intangible support—a good network and relevant advice

A Good Idea

By definition, entrepreneurial enterprises have "all their eggs in one basket." That basket had better be a good one.

The best way to come up with a great business idea is to observe and solve a real problem. Most successful entrepreneurs draw their ideas from personal experience. A study of America's five hundred fastest-growing companies found that 57 percent of the founders got the idea by seeing problems in the industry they had worked in before founding the company.[11] Ideas may also emerge from your experiences as a consumer:

something that you've been dissatisfied with that you could address more effectively, or something you care deeply about.

Your voices

Becky Minard and her husband Paal Gisholt are the founders of SmartPak, a rapidly growing company that provides horse and dog owners with leading name-brand supplements custom-packed in a patented unit-dose package.

My idea came from my frustration with the way my own horse was being cared for. I kept thinking that there *must* be a better way. My frustration helped me come up with the idea for the product and how it would work. It was also clear to me that I needed an outlet for my creativity.[12]

Steven Kramer cofounded College Coach, a business that provides college counseling services as an employee benefit, purchased by corporations for their employees' children. Recently, he and his partner successfully sold the business to Bright Horizons.

I care about creating a change within education. I wanted to impact people's lives. Our services open up college opportunities to people who might not have been able to afford it before. We give them greater alternatives. There are not many for-profit education opportunities out there, so if I wanted to be in that field, I had to start something on my own.[13]

Today's new technologies provide the basis for many entrepreneurial ventures. These five questions, based on principles of the emerging new economy and the resources suggested in the notes for each, will stimulate your thinking.[14]

1. *Can you enhance the development of or extract more value from tacit knowledge?* Perhaps the hottest area today is the application

of Web 2.0 technology to improve the productivity of high-value, knowledge-intensive interactions, those requiring expertise and judgment. Technology tools such as wikis, virtual team environments, and video-conferencing remove the need to spend time on activities that do not create value, ensure that workers have the right information at the right time, and capture insights in greater depth.[15]

2. *Can you combine data from multiple processes to automate more complex activities?* In the 1980s and 1990s, there was a big focus on automating discrete processes: supply chain forecasting, enterprise resource planning, and customer relationship management. These systems can now be connected through common standards for exchanging data. The resulting cross-system information can be combined in new ways to automate an increasing array of activities, from inventory management to customer service.[16]

3. *Can you analyze data in new ways?* It's easier than ever to collect and compare data, allowing the development of new insights. Intel integrates a "prediction market" with regular short-term forecasting processes to build more accurate and less volatile estimates of demand. Toll-road operators are segmenting drivers and charging them different prices based on static conditions (such as time of day) and dynamic ones (traffic). Harrah's casinos mine customer data to target promotions and drive exemplary customer service.[17]

4. *Can you use information transparency as the basis for a new business?* The Internet brought greater transparency to many markets, from airline tickets to stocks, enabling new businesses like Expedia. Many other sectors provide similar opportunity.[18]

5. *Can you identify valuable "exhaust data"?* The digitization of processes and activities creates by-products or "exhaust data" that can be exploited for profit. A retailer with digital cameras to prevent shoplifting, for example, is creating a digital database

> of consumer behavior that could be used by vendors to reshape their merchandising approaches.[19]

Whatever you do, complete your homework—a lot of homework.

Your voices

> **I have an idea a week for starting a business. It drives my husband nuts! We do tons of research to understand our ideas and the options for addressing them deeply, calling on all our former consulting skills. Ask yourself hard questions about whether you have a product looking for a market or have actually solved a problem for someone. Understand your market in depth and make sure you are solving a real problem.[20]**

A Good Plan

Put a lot of time and energy into the creation of a good business plan. Outlines of the type of information to include, along with good samples, are easily available on the Internet. Alternatively, if possible, you may want to take a class in entrepreneurship, in large part so you can get real-time feedback from peers in the course.

Your voices

> **I turn forty-one tomorrow and I am currently working on my cubicle exit plan. I'm writing a business plan to head out on my own.**

Develop multiple ideas and/or multiple business-model variations on a similar idea. In many instances, the greatest innovation and most sustainable advantage come from the underlying business model or operational approach, the *way* you solve the problem. Consider these four questions.

1. *Can you solve the need—and reduce your risk—by organizing a network of other independent firms or individuals to participate in the innovation process for a new product or service?* Open innovation or cocreation harnesses the talents of various independent innovators—customers, suppliers, small specialist businesses, independent contractors. Think in terms of tapping others to offer insights, but create a governance process that allows your company to shape the innovation process. The online clothing store Threadless asks people to submit new designs for T-shirts and allows the community to vote for its favorites.[21]

2. *Can you produce the product or service by tapping into specialized free-agent talent?* Many activities from finance to marketing and IT to operations can be found anywhere, for example, an individual in Singapore or a small company in Italy. You can build a business integrating the work of an expanding number of outsiders. As you consider this option, look for new and innovative ways of shaping the talent management model. For example, TopCoder, a company that has created a network of software developers, allows customers to offer prizes to those who do the best job creating the desired software.[22]

3. *Can you address the need by allowing consumers to become producers?* Can you build a business model around "prosumption" (simultaneous production and consumption) and draw consumers into the actual production process? Consider OhMyNews, a popular South Korean online newspaper written by more than sixty thousand contributors or "citizen reporters."[23]

4. *Can you unbundle and use other firms' existing physical assets to create a new value proposition?* Many asset-intensive businesses—factories, warehouses, truck fleets, office buildings, data centers, IT networks, and so on—can be unbundled, disaggregating the capacity into components that can be managed cost effectively.[24]

> For the large company, selling unused capacity raises their utilization rates and returns on invested capital. This allows you to access resources and assets that might otherwise require a large fixed investment or significant scale to achieve competitive marginal costs.[25]

Prepare rough draft plans for *at least six business options,* even those that, on the surface, are unlikely to be as attractive as your first idea. Going through this step will help you understand the sensitivities of the idea you eventually choose. It will help you explore some of the trade-offs, particularly ones that will increase your eventual speed to market, a key determinant of success.

Assemble (not necessarily physically, although sometimes a good face-to-face discussion helps) a group of people to critique your plans. This again is the advantage of taking a class. You end up with a built-in group of people who are all interested in entrepreneurship and can help you assess your ideas. But, however you do it, find ways to discuss your ideas with others.

Your voices

We really hammered out the business model. We took the process of writing a business plan very seriously. At the time, no one was focused on innovative services; we had to distinguish ourselves among all the excitement created by the Internet boom. One thing that worked well was being open about things, talking to Boomers who had done it before.[26]

Once you've narrowed down your options to one or two that look the most promising, develop a more detailed version of the plan that can guide your actions and measure your progress during the first critical years.

Your voices

What are the milestones that must be achieved within a certain time period? What numbers of customers do you need at various points? You need to pilot your services in ways that are measurable, so you can refine them over time. Use your business plan as a living document.[27]

If you're stuck in the planning stage, consider hiring other entrepreneurs to help you through this important step. There are firms that help busy professionals start businesses, while you remain at your current job.

Tangible Resources—The Right Skills and Enough Money

With a great business plan in hand, you should be in a good position to determine the tangible resources such as types of skills and the amount of initial funding you need to assemble to make the venture viable. Clearly, deep domain skills—competence in areas at the core of your business concept—are critically important. Make sure you have the talent and knowledge in the field or have access to them to create the maximum value for the enterprise.

However, in an entrepreneurial venture you also have to be a jack of all trades. You need to understand enough about all the activities required to make a company work so that you are sure of getting good value from others. This includes *everything*: finance and marketing, human resource issues like compensation and employee benefits, physical infrastructure issues like office space and telecommunications, and many others.

Your voices

One of the hardest parts was that neither I nor my partner had ever worked in an entrepreneurial company. We'd never been exposed to the nuts and bolts—things like payroll and rent.[28]

If you're short in key areas, try to assemble a team that will fill in the gaps. If you're not planning to make an entrepreneurial move soon, make obtaining the broad set of skills you'll need a goal for your remaining years of corporate life. Seek lateral moves designed to broaden your understanding of a wide range of business skills. The skills and talents you'll need may extend beyond those directly involved in the operating processes. For example, SmartPak's success hinged on endorsements from prominent equestrians who use the products to care for their horses.[29]

Many entrepreneurs choose to go into business with friends or family to ensure that they will be surrounded by people they trust and with whom they know they can collaborate. SmartPak grew out of the strong partnership between Becky and her husband, each of whom brought complementary skills to the venture.

Your voices

My desire to try out some of my own ideas and Paal's desire to run something kept cropping up. He had the venture capital connections and the ability to raise capital. I understood the market. We are both control freaks and perfectionists. We're good at project management and time lines. Now we just had to do it.[30]

Of course, beyond skills comes money. Should you try to bootstrap your venture? Most experienced entrepreneurs recommend raising some outside capital. Taking on an investor enforces structure by making you accountable and requiring that you think with discipline.[31] However, because a bad financial partner can be disastrous, make sure you choose financing from a reputable investor who understands your business.[32]

Intangible Support—A Good Network and Relevant Advice

A strong network of personal contacts and a willingness to seek advice are important for entrepreneurial success.

Your voices

Definitely seek out advisers. We had a lot of advisers. We asked individuals we knew could help in a way that was meaningful for advice and counsel—people who had good solid business experience. We were never afraid to ask people for their opinions. I learned in my consulting experience that a team always came up with better answers than any individual. Getting the right network together is a really important piece of the success.[33]

Before you begin an entrepreneurial venture, get to know people who will be able to help you later on, not only people with access to capital, although that's key, but people with related experience that you can turn to for advice.

Some of you undoubtedly think that you'll never choose this option. Here's one X'er who began with that view.

Your voices

Jean Ayers had just turned forty when she sent her first comments.

First communication: I have been working at the same organization for twelve years . . . It's a great place to work, which is why I'm still here. I love the people I work with . . . it's a highly respected "brand" (the name counts). Oh, and I have work/life balance. I don't want to work seventy-plus hours a week, unless of course I'm working to save lives, which I'm clearly not.

The question that plagues me is: is this all there is? I'm already forty years old. I'm not doing work that *really* matters (see the "saving lives" comment above). Intellectually, I realize that what matters are all the little things we continually do in life, like helping a friend, being there for your family, saying please and thank you. However, I feel like I still need to do something *big*. Shouldn't what I do leave a positive mark on the world? . . . What will *my* legacy be? I hope that at the very least, I'll be remembered as a good person who did the best she could. But am I? Am I doing my best?

In addition to all this existential angst, I often fantasize about chucking it all and traveling around the world, just meeting interesting people, writing, exploring, not worrying about mundane everyday things, and getting off the gerbil wheel. I dream of being my own boss (very Gen X of me, don't you think?). But, to be totally honest, I'm too chicken. I'm definitely *not* a risk taker . . . I'm not ready to give up my condo, my car, or my cat to be footloose and fancy free. Security is extremely important to me.

Should I move on? And, if so, why haven't I? Is it because my career has actually become less important to me as I've gotten older and it really is "all those little things" that I'm enjoying more and more and are taking over a bigger part of my life? Maybe . . . What holds me back is the fear that I'll lose that work/life balance I've achieved. Or that I'll just fail. So I struggle with my external desire to save the world with an internal desire to save my own life.[34]

12 months later: An update on where I am in my life. I finally did quit my job to move on to be the VP of marketing for a very cool online company . . . But after eight months, I've decided that it's not what I want to be doing with my life. So I'm taking another leap, this time to start my own business (and work as an online marketing consultant on the side). The business is one that I've been thinking about for, oh, about seven years or so. It will combine adventure travel with volunteering. I figure that if I'm going to work this hard for something, I should be doing something I feel passionate about. Am I hoping to save the world this time? Probably not, but I'm getting closer to feeling good about my particular role in it. Reviewing my original note really made me feel better about my decision to leave where I am now and embark on the rest of life.[35]

How do you feel about the option of becoming an entrepreneur?

Your voices

Many X'ers were forced at some point in their careers to try it on their own. And a good portion of them found it to be a better path than returning to corporate life. We're in control. If it succeeds, we get the profit. If it fails, it's our fault, and that's good too . . . My career is no longer at the risk of corporate issues . . . And none of this would be happening now if corporate had worked like it was supposed to. Glad it didn't. Happier now. Busier. And much more in control of my life.

Portfolio Careers

For many of you, the smartest move is to keep several back-up options in play. Back-ups are jobs you take on in addition to your "career job," based on your concern for the sustainability of your career, a desire to optimize income, or the need for greater flexibility.

Your voices

I'm thirty-three. The year I got married I worked for three different employers. Back-up plans aren't just something I like, they're a necessity for survival . . . My wife and I have a small business we run on the side. It kept us afloat when we were both in between jobs. Now it supports her. My wife sets her own hours, gets to stay home with our son, and she makes more than any employer was ever willing to pay her. What's not to like? I think going into business is a very good option for Gen X'ers. We have great ideas, and corporations generally don't want to hear them, which presents a great opportunity to compete with them.

We do work hard. We have skills and knowledge. Heck, we have lots and lots of ideas, as evidenced by our many entrepreneurial ventures. Everyone I know has a side project, and many of us are self-employed or small business owners.

Long ago I started considering myself a consultant, not an employee, and am always working on plans B and C, especially as I send more and more jobs to India. Despite being a change leader, there's little chance of me making VP at my *Fortune* 1000 company: Boomers are burrowed in and we'll all likely be outsourced anyway. Besides, if I did make VP, I'm not sure that for the 15 percent raise, it's worth giving up knowing my three young children. So I'm working on starting my own businesses on the side, cutting back on hours to do so, and am also looking at a part-time PhD program to become a university professor. Self-preservation. But this is just what I have to do to ensure I can support my family. It's not a conspiracy, just changing demographics and globalism. These are my realities to face.

I have the back-up plan. My husband and I run a small property management business and a seasonal greenhouse business in addition to our career jobs. We find it hard to give up the back-up plans, as we continue to be unsure of the sustainability of our mainstream jobs. Right now, we are focused on milking our earning potential as much as possible for the next ten years, then we are likely jumping out of the game.

For many of you, these back-up jobs are a prelude for a future career change—a way to lay the groundwork. Depending on the type of business you're starting, there may not be much you can actually do during the start-up phase. For example, if a programmer needs to code, your continued work on the specifications would just slow the process down.

Those who've gone the entrepreneurial route would agree that holding on to your corporate job as long as possible is a great way to minimize the risk and to ease in.

Keep these considerations in mind if you're thinking about a portfolio career.

- Don't suboptimize by trying to do so many things that you're not able to do any of them well.
- Make sure the "tempos" work together, that is, that the businesses have different "crunch points."
- Build in contingency time, if at all possible. Things will go wrong.
- Apply the same rigor to each business that I described earlier for starting an entrepreneurial venture. Conduct market research, do good planning, enlist advisers, and so on.

Explore and Experiment

There are many interesting opportunities outside the structure of big organizations. Think in terms of fifty or more years of active life. Use your time now to put yourself in a position to make the most of the future.

Herminia Ibarra, a professor of leadership and learning at INSEAD, has found in her research on how adults change careers that "events in their lives and work led them to envision a new range of *possible selves,* the various images—both good and bad—of whom we might become . . ."[36] She goes on to suggest, "For starters, we must reframe the questions, abandoning the conventional career-advice queries—'Who am I?'—in favor of more open-ended alternatives. Among the many possible selves that I might become, which is most intriguing to me now? Which is easiest to test?"[37]

Even if you aren't ready to launch new businesses, invest some time to explore and experiment.[38]

- *Explore*—Experience new people and ideas in ways that will uncover the possibilities. To find an interesting path, put yourself in interesting places in contact with interesting people and experience the shifts in behavior and attitudes under way in the world. Staying only within intimate circles of close friends and family may not present a full palette of alternatives; these relationships tend to preserve stability and familiarity. Instead, use your network's loose ties to discover new opportunities.

- *Experiment*—Try new things in small steps. Almost no one gets it right the first time or in one big step. Finding new, satisfying activities is an iterative process. Try something new, evaluate how well it really fits with your needs and preferences, and take another step. The key is taking action. Richard Pascale, a noted authority on organizational change, and his coauthors Mark Milleman and Linda Gioja pointed out in *Surfing the Edge of Chaos,* "Adults are much more likely to act their way into a new way of thinking than to think their way into a new way of acting."[39] As Ibarra advises, "Devote the greater part of [your] time and energy to action rather than reflection, to doing instead of planning."[40]

Whatever you do, if you find that your corporate work life is not all that it's cracked up to be, don't allow yourself to be bored or frustrated. Find another path that will lead to a more satisfying life.

CHAPTER EIGHT

The NeXt Generation Leader

Why You're What We Need Now . . . and How

The generations preceding you have made their contributions to the state of today's business and the world. They've brought blends of energy and idealism, optimism and some arrogance, productivity and occasional greed. They've built major institutions, most based largely on a hierarchical model, command-and-control approaches, an assumption that information could be proprietary, and rules that dictated a zero-sum outcome.

We've made some remarkable social and economic progress under that leadership. Perhaps most striking, we've achieved greater racial tolerance and gender equality. Unprecedented opportunities in many parts of the world are bringing millions of people into the global economic sphere.

These strong pluses are offset by a number of pressing and complex concerns. Meanwhile, the very advances in technology that make new opportunities possible are bringing challenges to the fore, making it increasingly possible for those on the edge to voice their ideas, as well as their anger and frustration.

Future leaders in all spheres will have to contend with a world with finite limits, no easy answers, and the sobering realization that we are facing significant, seemingly intractable problems on multiple fronts. Perhaps the biggest change from past models: leaders will have to listen and respond to diverse points of view. There will be no dominant voice.

William Strauss and Neil Howe, coauthors of *Generations,* posit that each generation makes a unique bequest to those that follow and generally seeks to correct the excesses of the previous generation. They argue that the Boomer excess is ideology and that the Generation X reaction to that excess involves an emphasis on pragmatism and effectiveness.[1] This generational priority will give you a strong advantage in remaking organizations to reflect twenty-first century realities: the need for transparency, accountability, real-time performance, lack of ideology, top-of-market effectiveness, and cash value.[2]

I'm convinced that Gen X'ers will be the leaders we need in other ways as well. Your awareness of global issues was shaped in your youth, and you are richly multicultural. You bring a more unconscious acceptance of diversity than any preceding generation. Your formative years followed the civil rights advances of the 1960s. High divorce rates during your youth meant you are the first generation to grow up with women in independent authority roles. The most difficult elements of your past may well be those that provide you with the strongest capabilities for today.

Your voices

Born in 1970, I resent the misfortunes which seem to have compromised Gen X at key moments: recessions, debt, AIDS, and divorce . . . However, the most positive attributes of X'ers to emerge from this experience include flexibility, articulation, vision, and resilience . . . I think X'ers make perfect management material right now, capable of better medium- and long-term decisions that will protect all three generations.

You have traded idealism for realism, tempered by value-oriented sensibilities that will help you serve as effective stewards of both today's organizations and tomorrow's world. As such, you will become the pragmatic mid-life managers of the crisis: economic, environmental, political, military, or cultural, applying toughness and resolution to defend society while safeguarding the interests of the young. You will force the nation to produce more than it consumes and fix the infrastructure.[3] Strauss and Howe observe: "Every tool acquired during a hardened childhood and individualist youth will be put to maximum test."[4]

Your voices

The problem with the Boomer generation is they really believed in utopia. And utopia is dead . . . We understand crisis. So we're pissed off, and we understand that utopia doesn't work.[5]

Your skepticism and ability to isolate practical truths will help you redefine issues and question reality. Even your humor will be an asset. Czech leader Václav Havel said, "There are no exact guidelines. There are probably no guidelines at all. The only thing I can recommend at this stage is a sense of humor, an ability to see things in their ridiculous and absurd dimensions, to laugh at others and at ourselves, a sense of irony regarding everything that calls out for parody in this world."[6]

You will have the opportunity to change the corporate template and create organizations that are more conducive to your values. As leaders, you will be able to reshape the organizations you lead to make them better places for future generations and yourselves, make them more humane, and break the cultural norms of corporate life—long hours, a focus on full-time work, heterogeneous perspectives, and language of combat.[7] You will bring your desire to create better alternatives, including how to balance work with commitments beyond the corporation and find meaning in work. Most importantly, your preference for "alternative" and your inclination to innovate will allow you to look for a different way forward.

Your voices

I think the things the Gen X'ers learned are extremely valuable in times of great socioeconomic and political chaos. You are doing a great thing by turning the focus back to this generation after we "stealthed" our way through our short and inglorious legacy within the corporate rank and file. Wow! I had almost forgotten we existed.

This chapter is about you in the role of leaders, whether you are leading through influence, managing people within a unit or group, taking on the challenge of transforming a traditional corporation, founding a business of your own, or working through organizations aimed at broader societal needs.

The chapter covers a broad spectrum of challenges, because the years between your early thirties and mid- to late forties are ones of great change, the highest velocity, in all likelihood, in your career. Younger X'ers may just be entering the first lines of leadership, while many older X'ers already fill important senior roles. Nonetheless, the principles of leadership derived from your generation's sensibilities and the needs posed by today's complex environment are surprisingly the same. At multiple levels, the challenge remains one of innovation, collaboration, diversity, and engagement.

Your voices

We've got the raw materials to do something . . . We're equipped. We're wary enough to see through delusional "movements"; we're old enough to feel a connection to the past (and yet we're unsentimental enough not to get all gooey about it); we're young enough to be wired; we're snotty enough not to settle for crap; we're resourceful enough to turn crap into gold; we're quiet enough to endure our labors on the margins; we're experienced enough to know that change *begins* on the margins. Beyond that, *we're all we got.*[8]

A Model for Leadership Today

Perhaps we need a new word. *Roget's Thesaurus* provides the following synonyms for *leadership*: administration, authority, command, control, direction, domination, foresight, guidance, hegemony, influence, initiative, management, power, preeminence, primacy, skill, superintendency, superiority, supremacy, sway.[9] We have come to expect a leader to be out in front, to know where we're going, and to supply all the answers.

These current leadership norms were honed in a different environment, largely a Traditionalist world in which it was easier to view one position as right and the other wrong and easier to predict, forecast, and control. Most standard wisdom advises that you lead during challenges by increasing control—review your costs, tighten your approval criteria, pull key decisions and sign-offs up to higher levels and narrow the business scope.

This model may not settle comfortably for many of you. I'll argue shortly that it's not what's needed anyhow.

Your voices

X'ers will never get to leadership positions because we have no ability or desire to tell others what to do. We were not groomed for leadership by parents, teachers, or bosses and are more than a little shocked and angry when expected to pay for or clean up other people's messes . . . All we Gen X'ers can do is smile pretty, edit the documents, and build our little happy lives through cultivating our garden à la Voltaire.

I would throw out one more reason for our exodus from corporate leadership: Boomer executives expect us to act and think like they do . . . In other words, after years of learning under their wise leadership, we're now "mature" enough to understand and embrace the idea that

layoffs are just a part of doing business, that people must be thought of as "resources," and that it's only natural for individuality to be suborned by corporate culture. It's only now that we've been molded appropriately that we can be permitted to take up the reins of executive leadership. Is it any wonder some of us reject the idea that we are destined to live in the shadows of their ideals, rather than applying our own ideas and viewpoints in leading organizations?

Not only do the approaches of the past fail to match X'er sensibilities, they are unlikely to work for many organizational challenges. There are too many uncertainties for any of us to feel confident that we can predict how this game will play out. The complex and ambiguous conditions of the first quarter of this century are unlikely to respond to the old school of leadership. You're becoming leaders when the demands of leadership are changing, in ways that, to a large extent, mirror your values and experience.

Ronald Heifetz, a professor at the Harvard Kennedy School, has argued that a different type of leadership is required for complex contemporary problems than for routine problems. The latter requires expertise (manifested through knowledge and experience), while leadership for what he calls *adaptive* problems, such as the complex issues of crime, poverty, and educational reform (and to which I would add a wide range of global political, environmental, and political crises) requires skill in both *innovation* and the *consideration of values*.[10] Heifetz and his colleague R. M. Sinder call for a future form of leadership that provides a *context* in which all interested parties, the leader included, can together create a vision, mission, or purpose they can collectively uphold.[11]

Many of the problems we face today in business and beyond are adaptive. Your leadership will be about creating a context of adaptability in the face of ambiguity to help organizations become more spontaneous and reflexive. Innovation will be the lifeblood of the organization and proof of the success of your leadership. To create an environment that supports innovation, you, as a leader, will play a catalytic role with five essential context-creating responsibilities:

1. *Increase collaborative capacity*. Leaders must heighten the likelihood that knowledge will be exchanged by developing trust-based relationships throughout the organization. The shift is away from relationships that are primarily to and through you; instead you become a catalyst for creating relationships among others.

2. *Ask compelling questions*. Leaders must rally the organization around goals that are intriguing, complex, and important. The shift is away from the leader as the source of answers to the leader as the framer of powerful challenges.

3. *Embrace complexity and seek disruptive information*. Rather than simplifying, ensure that you and your organization are open to ambiguous, uncomfortable, and contradictory information. The shift is away from control, prediction, and forecasting to sensing and holding open multiple possibilities.

4. *Shape identity*. Reflect your core values in the way the organization operates; distinguish it from others that might appear similar on the surface. Be authentic with customers, suppliers, and employees. Attract people who are predisposed to enjoy working in your organization. The shift is away from best-practice uniformity to expressing organizational and personal idiosyncrasy as a way to enhance engagement across all constituencies.

5. *Appreciate diversity*. Be open to multiple points of view. Recognize that your own view is one perspective among many and is influenced by your background. The shift is away from a zero-sum, right-and-wrong world to one of many rational possibilities.

Later in this chapter, I'll offer some tactical suggestions for leading, whether your role is positional, project-based, or influential. But first, more on these five responsibilities.

Increase Collaborative Capacity

Strong, trust-based relationships are the foundation for the behaviors you need both as an individual and within the organization you lead. These relationships are essential for collaboration, which in turn is needed to bring ideas together to innovate and to address complex challenges.

Think about innovations from which you've benefited in the past. Did you know that Post-it Notes were developed when one colleague's research failure—glue that didn't work well—solved another colleague's frustration with keeping his page markers secure in his choir book? Or that Nike running shoes were developed jointly by a coach with an in-depth understanding of runners' feet and a boot maker with the skill to craft a new type of shoe?

In these examples, and many others that I've studied over the years, innovation occurred when two areas of knowledge or insight came together. The most straightforward definition of innovation is, in some way, the combination of two previously unrelated ideas. These might be an insight about a business need and a new way to solve it, two technologies that have never before been combined, the skills of one colleague sparking the creativity of another, or any other merger of two approaches or perspectives.

Occasionally, disparate ideas come together within one individual's mind, perhaps as the result of a highly unusual combination of personal knowledge, experience, and exposure. But more often, creative leaps are sparked by two or more people working together, each with their own unique competency, perspectives, and experiences. The paradox is this: although such diversity is the foundation of disparate ideas, it is also the very thing that is most likely to *discourage* knowledge sharing. Most of us find it much more difficult to form trust-based relationships with people we perceive as being "different."[12] Not that these relationships don't happen, but they typically take longer to form and require greater focus and intent. Diversity decreases the likelihood of knowledge transfer *unless* you purposely invest in forming relationships.

Creating the capacity to bring ideas together on a reliable, consistent basis depends on ensuring that multiple individuals will freely exchange knowledge. This requires strong, safe relationships between people. As a contemporary leader, one of your primary responsibilities is to build your organization's capacity for collaboration by systematically investing in activities that develop trust-based relationships. Because, as a generation, you operate comfortably with diversity and value relationships, you are suited to this challenge. As you share your habits and skills, you will help others throughout the organizations you lead.

Leaders in organizations with significant capacity to collaborate and innovate actively set the stage:[13]

- *Invest in networks around innovation priorities.* Collaboration, as I'm using it here, requires an investment of time and effort from the people involved. It is the act of working together, especially in a joint intellectual effort. It has nothing to do with being "nice," per se. And not all tasks require it.

Determine which parts of the organization need to exchange insights and whether the collaborative capacity among members of those groups is strong. Do the *right* people know and trust each other?[14]

- *Select people who like to collaborate.* If collaboration is important to a program's success, gauge an individual's preference for doing so as part of the selection and promotion processes.

- *Create a "gift" culture.* Establish an organizational culture in which people freely give their time to help others. Model this behavior personally; share the best of yourself by becoming a teacher, a mentor, and a mentee. Focus on developing others. Be open to what you can learn from those younger. Visible examples of senior leaders generously helping and learning from others are a powerful way to spread this behavior.

- *Design ways to format trust-based relationships.* Make significant and thoughtful investments in programs and processes that will facilitate the development of relationships. Approaches can vary widely, including:

- Events to give people opportunities to meet
- Technology to allow work groups to communicate easily
- Education to strengthen people's ability to resolve conflict and hold meaningful conversations
- Physical architecture to provide informal space for colleagues to congregate
- Organizational design to create units of a size that permit people to know each other and understand the whole and negate the need for excessive control[15]
- Process or workflow design to consider relationship formation by bringing people together regularly during the process.

- *Leverage strong relationships within the organization.* Nokia, for example, often transfers small groups of employees or pods from one area to another so that they begin each new job with already formed relationships. And, when budgets are tight, don't eliminate the meetings that are key to forming relationships, intensify the competition among internal teams, or reduce investments in learning, not if you plan to innovate.
- *Operate as a community of adults.* Trust the people you lead. Establish practices, particularly for access to and handling of sensitive information, that signal the organization's trust of employees. In a possibly extreme example, the Brazilian company Semco has done away with expense reports. CEO Ricardo Semler's view is that requiring the reports implies that you are questioning either whether the worker actually incurred the expense or the individual's judgment in doing so, in either case, diminishing the sense of trust.[16]
- *Make sure processes are efficient, tasks are well managed, and roles are clearly defined.* Collaboration is seriously compromised by processes

that waste participants' time and by unclear and ambiguous role definitions that force people to parry over authority and control. The leader's responsibility is to provide clear, well-structured roles.

- *Leave the approach itself to the discretion and creativity of the team.* Tasks that are too tightly prescribed inhibit collaboration and innovation. Why bother, if there's little latitude in the approach? Think of the emergency room in a hospital as the model of clear roles and ambiguous tasks. The role definitions among the team members are precise. When beginning work on a new patient, there's no need for discussion about who would like to do the surgery that day. However, the nature of the challenge—what will be wrong with the patient and therefore what steps will be required for treatment—is unknown, and the precise steps required are therefore ambiguous.

Ask Compelling Questions

Great leaders pose great questions that are ambitious, and novel. They frame intriguing, memorable, essential, and worthy challenges that ignite the organization. This responsibility represents perhaps the most significant departure from conventional views of leadership. The leader's role shifts from making key decisions to posing questions that allow broad participation in forming a response. Use your expertise, wisdom, and intelligence to shape better questions, to discern trends earlier, to frame more intriguing challenges, and to articulate them in compelling ways.

Asking great questions is particularly important for innovation, but it means giving up some of the traditional notions of the leader's power and the norm of imposing top-down edicts. There are few things more likely to stifle any hint of innovation—to freeze people in their tracks—than to *command* that they "innovate." Leaders who make statements like "5 percent of our revenue *must* come from new products"—are almost certainly dampening the organization's ability to respond.

In contrast, John F. Kennedy's ambitious and intriguing goal for space exploration was an inspiring challenge: "This nation should commit itself to achieving the goal, before this decade is out, of landing a man on the Moon and returning him safely to the Earth."[17] The goal brought the scientific community together in an exciting collaborative quest to solve a seemingly insurmountable technical challenge.

Robert Shapiro, when he became the CEO of Monsanto, issued a similar challenge. Rather than exhorting people to "be more innovative," Shapiro spoke about the powerful new developments in biotechnology and the pressing need to address the problems of world hunger. He challenged the organization with the intriguing question of whether Monsanto might use biotechnology to solve some of the world's food shortages. His challenge inspired tremendous collaboration throughout the firm, resulting in thousands of suggestions for new, innovative solutions.[18]

Both are examples of a leader rallying an organization around what I call "intent"—a powerfully worded question or goal. Like the idea of "strange attractors" in chaos theory, intent becomes a touchstone that drives people toward new levels of creativity and commitment, a galvanizing force to align people around the new challenge.

Embrace Complexity and Seek Disruptive Information

Acknowledge complexity head on, without attempting to minimize the difficulties or ambiguities. Research has found that ignoring or oversimplifying challenges does not work, largely because of the stress it places on the organization, which quickly sees through the facade. Leaders are responsible for grappling honestly with complex issues.[19] Your generation's shared tendency to reject absolutes, to accept that there is no final "right" analysis of events that tops all other analyses, no single rationality, no universal morality, no crisp sound-bite solutions for multidimensional problems is a great asset.

This leadership responsibility also embodies seeking disruptive information and bad news. It requires challenging your own assumptions, absorbing new perspectives, adopting new technology, and exploring new ideas. And it means exposing the organization you lead to provocative thinking. Leaders must disrupt their stable system by ensuring that new insights are continually introduced. Pragmatic paths to diverse perspectives include:

- Hire mavericks
- Expose the organization to social, political, demographic, and technological trends
- Tap a wide range of problem solvers
- Explore thoughtful "what if" perspectives through scenario development and options analysis
- Feed the mind and the imagination with exercises to think more broadly and look at things in new and different light
- Arrange visits to other innovators, not only those in your industry or facing the same problems you face, but all types of innovative organizations

As you bring in new people and new ideas, you'll need to deal with the paradox I discussed earlier. Because the people who are the most likely to share information are the ones that know each other well, bringing in new people requires a continual investment in forming new relationships.

Shape Identity

Leaders are often asked to express their "vision"; and their answers are often found lacking. It's difficult to articulate a vision—whatever you think that word means—that touches the chord people are looking to have struck. In reality, when we ask that question, we are rarely looking for a business school–type articulation of an organizational strategy.

Vision is a code word for *identity*. People want to know what the identity of the organization is—what ties the people within it together. What makes being a member of this organization unique?

Addressing this human longing—shaping identity—is an essential leadership responsibility. It encompasses many of the traditional ideas about leading people—motivation, attraction, retention—but in a way that reflects the leader's values and the organization's unique characteristics. It is an orientation based on authenticity and, as such, a comfortable fit for most Gen X'ers.

Conveying a strong identity has tremendous benefit. You attract and retain people who like what it means to work in your organization. This expression of personality and differentiation draws people to specific organizations and engages them in that organization's purpose. It creates a greater sense of commitment, pride and enthusiasm—of engagement with the organization and its work. The following are some ways you as a leader can shape identity and create engagement in your organization.

Identify what it means to work in your organization and with you

Organizations with a strong identity are not all things to all people. The experience of working in one is likely to appeal to some people more than to others. These organizations exemplify the personal values of their leaders, past and present. The leaders know what the experience of working in the organization is like for employees. They recognize that individuals work for different reasons and, by demonstrating or describing the employee experience accurately and vividly, attract employees who are predisposed to like what the organization has to offer.

Consider the organization you lead and reflect on the following:

- What values are most important to you personally?
- What is your organization's greatest distinction? What elements of the overall employee experience do you handle in somewhat unique ways?

- What do you offer more of than other organizations who compete for the same talent you do?
- What is the best part of the current employee experience? Why do employees say they like working here?
- What do you tell candidates who are considering joining your firm? What is your value proposition? What do you promise? Do your colleagues describe the same value proposition and know the same stories you do?
- Do you use any stories or examples to describe what working in your company is like?

Consider, too, how the business environment is changing and whether you can realistically continue to offer the value proposition that you have been using successfully.

Assess current and future employees' values and preferences

A strong sense of identity, leading to high levels of employee engagement, depends on the match between what an individual really enjoys about work and what experience a company can realistically provide.

Consider these questions when evaluating your employees' values:

- What do your current employees care about? Why did they join this organization? (Why did you?)
- What is their generational profile and underlying assumption about work?
- How are the organization's talent needs changing? How do the people you will need tomorrow differ from those you have today? What might future employees care about?
- Can you identify an unmet employment need, either within the firm or in the external labor market?

- Are you able to address your employees' preferences in a distinctive and compelling way? What can you offer that is better than what any competitor offers?

If you need to shift your value proposition to attract and retain a different type of individual, meet the change head on. Discuss with employees what the organization can now offer and begin to create a realistic employee experience that is strong and unique in its own way. Although some current employees may elect to leave, in most cases, that's preferable to those who stay in body only, those who just can't connect with the organization's identity, typically resulting in disastrously low levels of engagement. Some will change along with you, allowing you to update their sense of identity as the organization evolves.

Showcase your organization's distinctive characteristics

Help people decide for themselves whether this is a place they want to be part of. Encourage intelligent adults to make decisions about whether your organization is a good fit for them.

Your voices

Today the culture at our company is laid back and casual, but with an intense work ethic. We're all about speed and efficiency, not so much about face time. It's a reflection of my personality, all about getting things done fast and well. When candidates interview, we focus on telling them how *bad* it can get here—how crazy it is at times—to see if that type of environment appeals to them. Of course we're delighted when we find the right candidate and they accept, but we also count the interview as a success if the candidate chooses not to join. If candidates weed themselves out because of our frankness, it saves us quite a bit of time because a rough-and-tumble start-up isn't the right fit for many people.[20]

It makes sense to encourage prospective employees to evaluate fit for themselves. Remember the story of Zappos, a company that pays people to quit (see chapter 5)? Other successful firms use different approaches to signal early on what the employee experience will be like. The key is making sure that your organization's identity is sufficiently clear so that prospective employees can understand for themselves what it's like to work there.

One of the best ways to communicate an organization's values is by developing what I call *signature experiences*—visible, distinctive elements of an organization's overall employee experience. A signature experience serves as a powerful, living example of the organization's culture, values, and heritage, making the characteristics of your employee experience more vivid. Signature experiences tend to be idiosyncratic and tricky for competitors to imitate, precisely because they have evolved in-house and reflect the company's heritage and the leadership team's ethos.

If your firm doesn't have a strong signature experience, it makes sense to develop one. Consider:

- What processes are most important to your firm's success? (If possible, make these your most distinct experiences.)
- What does it take to succeed at your firm? Is there a key skill set or behavioral pattern that most successful employees share? If so, can you embed these in a signature process that all employees would experience?
- Which decentralized decisions or process activities would you most like to standardize in a common set of values?
- Do the stories that surround the company's founding or earlier history still provide relevant lessons for today's business needs? Could they be actively applied to parts of the employee experience? Can any of these stories be amplified and extended into more powerful, widespread, and distinctive processes?
- What innovative signature experience would best communicate and reinforce "what it means to work here"? Think creatively!

Once you develop the organization's signature experiences, one of your most important roles is to talk about them. The lore stays alive—and becomes most powerful—when it is told and retold.

Your voices

I see my role today as one of maintaining the culture and telling the corporate story. How I started SmartPak, what we value and stand for. How we want to serve our customers and help them solve their problems.[21]

Reinforce with aligned best practices

Have you ever had something occur in an organization—perhaps a new management policy—that that seems out of sync with what you'd expect? Perhaps the firm introduces a compensation system based on individual performance when all the other processes are geared to promote teamwork. Practices that are not aligned with the organization's identity jar employees' sense of what it means to work there. My research shows that one of the most common causes of low engagement is employees' perception that some elements of the work experience aren't exactly as they were advertised.

Leaders need to ensure a consistent employee experience throughout the organization:

- Is there any aspect of the current employee experience that doesn't seem to "fit" people's expectations or preferences? What surprises them the most during their first three months after hire? What are the most irritating elements of the employee experience for most employees?
- Are you offering elements of the employee experience that few, if any, of your employees really care about? Are there opportunities

to do less in some areas? Could you free up resources to shift to areas of higher impact?

- What experiments would allow you to explore alternative approaches?

Organizations—even very large ones—don't need to be all things to all people. In fact, they shouldn't try. You can attract people who are suited to your organization's culture and interested in furthering its goals. Conversely, you must be willing to accept that your employment proposition won't appeal to everyone. Communicate your organization's identity to convince the *right* people—those intrigued and excited by the work environment you offer, and who will reward you with their loyalty—to choose you.

Appreciate Diversity

As complexity increases, successful leaders will be those who appreciate the "rightness" of multiple positions and the way individuals' differing values influence their views and behaviors. (One of the major goals of this book is to help explain why X'ers *are* right, as are Boomers and Y's, based on the events and ideas that shaped their lives.) This leadership responsibility requires a more subtle appreciation of diversity than has been required of past leaders. We are moving beyond political correctness—not offending or harassing those with diverse perspectives—to acknowledge that the existence of differences is vital to fully appreciate an issue and its possible outcomes.

An even more sophisticated challenge is to recognize your built-in biases. Everyone's point of view—yours and the other guy's—reflect your particular lens and is therefore necessarily partial and incomplete. Acknowledging that there is no reason *any* individual's perspective should be given primary significance or value—even if you are the leader—gives you the ability to evaluate multiple points of view.

Diversity of perspective, of course, derives from many sources, generational differences being only one. For many organizations, however, generational differences are proving particularly challenging. Often we are not as sensitive to those differences as we might be of other, more traditional forms of diversity. It's easy to form a negative impression of "those old guys" or "those kids" and, interestingly, more socially acceptable to express unflattering stereotypes of other generations than it would be to condemn those from another race, gender, or nationality. (Could you imagine labelling someone from another race or gender with the words we often hear applied to other generations: "slacker" or "the dumbest generation," for example?)

Part of a leader's responsibility is to help bridge the generational divide.

Leading Across the Ages

A straightforward, effective way to help multigenerational groups work together effectively is to establish ground rules or norms for issues frequently viewed differently by each generation that easily lead to misunderstandings. Discussing the differences and agreeing on a workable approach will help head off potential conflicts.

The widest gaps in perceptions across the generations are driven by:

- *The meaning of "work" and its implications for how members of each generation view time and place.* Many members of older generations began their careers when work was the time one spent in the office, visibly on the job. This view is a logical carryover from a manufacturing-based economy when employees had to *be* at the assembly line. In contrast, tech-immersed younger workers tend to view work as something you do *anywhere, any time* and find the rigidity of set work hours a throwback to another era. As a result, it's easy for individuals from different generations to misinterpret each other's behaviors regarding time and place. Is someone who starts work at 9:30 a.m. working less hard than other team members who start at 8:30? Does it *matter* whether people are working in the office, at home, or somewhere else? Does everybody have to be in the workplace during the same hours to accomplish their tasks? Is doing so viewed by some as an important sign of team commitment?

- *How generations communicate and form relationships.* Preferred communication approaches can cause misunderstandings. You are much more comfortable using brief electronic communication than members of older generations may be. Y's are even more so; they may be annoyed if messages are not answered quickly. On the other hand, not only might team members from older generations be uncomfortable with digital communication; they may feel offended by a lack of face-to-face interaction. Agree on group norms for the types of information you'll share or discussions you'll hold via e-mail versus in person. Clarify expectations regarding appropriate response times.

- *How generations sync up.* Figuring out how to get together can be a challenge among generations. Older generations are planners and schedulers; Gen Y's are coordinators. Boomers are frequently very annoyed by younger team members' seemingly seat-of-the-pants approach. Y's often find their colleagues' reliance on prescheduled meetings and schedules inefficient and frustratingly slow.

- *How generations find information and learn new things.* Generations differ in the way they are most likely to approach new tasks and obtain the necessary information. Boomers and Traditionalists are linear learners. Most are inclined to attend training classes, read manuals, and absorb the requisite information from expert sources *before* beginning the task at hand. Gen Y's are largely "on demand" learners. They figure things out *as they go,* reaching out to the people who can give them the answers.

- *Job assignments.* The generations have different expectations for when and how frequently individuals will get plum new job assignments. In large part because of the "immediacy" I discussed earlier, Y's often look for these types of assignments right from the start. Boomer (and a good proportion of X'er) managers who fall back on arguments about the need to "pay your dues" run the risk of turning these energetic employees off.
- *The meaning of* feedback. *Feedback* has two meanings in today's workplace. Boomers expect that a "feedback discussion" with the boss will be an *assessment* of performance in which the boss renders a *judgment.* It's not something that occurs on a daily, weekly, or even monthly basis; once or twice a year is plenty. But, because Y's learn through personal interactions, a Y who says, "I'd like more feedback," is almost always expressing a desire to learn more. Y's hope you'll share ideas, input, suggestions, or coaching. People who comment that Y's "can't take criticism" are missing the point. It's not that they can't take it; it's that they're seeking something else. They are in a learning phase and are asking you to teach, not to score.

The key is not to declare any point of view right or wrong, but to surface and discuss openly any differences in expectations and ensure that everyone is comfortable with—or at least clearly understands—the agreed-on norms. As you lead people from different generations, be sensitive to differing expectations and preferences and, of course, to your own biases. Where on the spectrum do your preferences fall?

Beyond keeping an open mind and creating mutually agreed-on team norms, there are specific things you can do as you lead members of each generation.

Leading Generation Y

There's no question that leading Y's can be tough at times. But they're the team you've got, and they do have a number of strengths.

Your voices

I'm a thirty-five-year-old male X'er who has spent thirteen years in corporate. Just like all you other X'ers, I took my beatings. There is *no way* I want to somehow "punish" Gen Y for what Gen X had to endure. I remember the enthusiasm and new ideas I had as a recent grad. I remember being scoffed at and had work dumped on me as punishment for being an upstart. Perhaps I'm more romantic than some of my fellow X'ers, but I want to foster that drive and spirit in my younger coworkers. I know that they will need to be coached through the complexities of corporate America to understand that a solution that appears so simple to them is unworkable. America is all about innovation. Let's work *with* Gen Y to forge a corporate America that listens to employees, fosters communication between the generations, and institutes the most cost-effective, customer-focused improvements possible. Happy customers who see value in your product will provide your corporation with plenty of capital to reward shareholders *and* to train and encourage employees to improve the organization for the customers' benefit. It's called a cycle of prosperity, and Gen Y is ready for it.

Ten things to know about managing Ys:

1. Communicate in Y-friendly ways. Use their technology and approach, when possible, particularly during the recruiting process. Clarify when you expect them to use yours.

2. Address parents as an explicit part of your recruiting strategy. Gen Y's parents are an inevitable part of the process. Develop messages about why your organization is a great place for their child to work. Be prepared to respond to their concerns, to a reasonable degree.

3. Shift performance management to tasks, not time. Where possible, embrace time-shifting, asynchronous work, and flexible schedules.

4. Invest in technology and in your own technology skills. Try new approaches. Leverage technology to create efficient processes.

5. Coach first-line managers on the essentials of managing Y's. They do require more time than many other employees, largely because they're seeking managers willing to teach.

6. Foster knowledge sharing. Y's are surprised if they are not encouraged to reach out broadly for the input they need.

7. Encourage Boomers to mentor Y's. Y's like Boomers. Make your life easier by asking Boomers to serve as mentors and take on some of the teaching responsibilities.

8. Challenge Y's with tasks that require "figuring it out." Don't over-specify how to do the job.

9. Design career paths with frequent, lateral moves. They don't necessarily want to move up, but they'll stay more engaged if they have new things to do.

10. Provide world-class learning opportunities in all forms. The chance to learn is the number one thing Y's say they expect from their employer.

Managing Boomers

Managing those older than you, some of whom perhaps have been your former leaders, requires understanding Boomers, and more generally, "May–December" relationships.

One of my early mentors used the word *approbation* frequently. I don't hear it much these days, but he spoke often of having approbation for colleagues, those people he "had time for" and whose views he valued enough to consider thoughtfully. The dictionary defines *approbation* as "an expression of warm approval" and emphasizes that it is usually used in official relationships. Approbation is the key to forging a strong relationship between people of significantly different ages.

A reporting relationship between a younger boss and an older employee doesn't need to be awkward, but there can be complications. If the older worker is stepping down from a leadership position or feels competitive with the younger boss, that's obviously difficult. And Boomers, in particular, tend to be fairly competitive. They often appear to have a harder time ceding leadership than other generations do.

Your voices

As a Gen X'er (age thirty-four) in management, I'm struggling with how to navigate the generational divide. The Boomers above me are like Boomers have always been, born on third thinking they hit a triple and convinced that I haven't suffered enough to earn more money, respect, responsibility, or whatever.

Here are some tips for managing Boomers:

1. Ask questions. Avoid coming in with preconceived notions; listen carefully to the views of those in your group.
2. Go out of your way to signal that you recognize and respect the positive elements of "the way it has been done so far." Avoid implying that the old way has no value. It may need to change, but it's worth understanding why intelligent people have made the choices they have. Approach any change from the perspective that you will be adding to the strengths of the past, rather than repudiating the group's previous approaches.
3. Don't worry about "convincing" the other guy that you have the necessary skills and experience. *Demonstrate* that you do.
4. Develop a strong interpersonal relationship through a spirit of mutual approbation.

In addition, take the particular situation and characteristics of Boomers into account.

1. Retire *retirement*—Invite Boomers to stay, if they like. Recruit those who retired early and regret it now.

2. Create a variety of bell-shaped curve career options, including cyclic work and options that offer greater responsibility and that offer an opportunity to cut back.

3. Facilitate ways for giving back—Encourage Boomers to be active in mentoring, community service, and knowledge sharing.

4. Package new programs as a way to "win"—They're competitive! One company offered the option of cutting back as a "contest." Only those selected as the best would be allowed to cut back to more flexible roles. Boomers lined up in droves to apply for this popular approach.

Managing Gen X'ers

Leading other X'ers raises multiple considerations. You may be stepping out of a pool of peers to manage your former colleagues or people who may have applied for your job. You may have a team of people with as much or more experience than you. And you need to recognize the specific preferences and challenges facing your generation.

My suggestions for approbation and respect are important elements of addressing the first consideration. But managing peers often has a second dimension, shifting the nature of your relationship. There are no absolute rules for how closely to maintain a friendship with someone who is now a direct report; be thoughtful about how your actions affect the group as a whole. Guidelines about former rivals are a bit clearer: you cannot lead a group effectively if one or more members are behaving subversively. Your job is to create a clear invitation for full participation; their job is to decide if that works for them and, if not, to move along.

X'ers, specifically, have mistrusted authority, and now you're the authority. What would you want? Probably, more than anything, a sensible, respectful explanation and the option to weigh in. Author Michel Muetzel tells a story based on a television interview with the legendary football coach Bobby Bowden. Asked to describe the major differences between the young Boomer college players of twenty years ago and the Gen X players he was recruiting at that time, Bowden responded that when Boomers were told to run through the wall, they simply ran through the wall. The Gen X athletes were usually bigger, faster, and stronger than those of the past, but when asked to run through the wall, they wanted to know why. Only after getting an explanation of the importance of running through the wall, would they run through the wall. The concept of blind trust is gone forever.[22]

The following are additional tips for leading Generation X:

1. Design career paths that broaden career options, rather than narrow them.
2. Give individuals multiple choices and control over their career paths.
3. Look for ways to leverage your generation's entrepreneurial instincts, perhaps by sponsoring new venture activity.
4. Minimize requests for physical moves that sever social connections.
5. Provide family-friendly flexibility.
6. Create "on-ramps" for those who have stepped off the track in their thirties. Let them leave and help them return.
7. Invest in technology. Provide the time required to incorporate it.

Leadership Day-to-Day

Now to some of the more nitty-gritty tactics. For those of you who are just entering the leadership ranks, the initial step is likely to be delegation, sharing work with another colleague under your guidance.

One-on-One Leadership

Generation X entered the work world when hierarchies were flattening in many industries and the advent of personal technology was reducing the availability of personal assistants for mid- and lower-level staff. Many of you have not yet worked with someone else closely, to *delegate*. Some of you have mentioned that you feel guilty when you do or struggle with giving up control.

Delegating allows the people you lead to develop, and that's a huge part of your role. A simple model provides the framework for thinking about this experience and other leadership relationships you'll have going forward: integrate the needs of the individual and the needs of the organization. Delegate what the other person needs to learn in order to grow and/or the tasks that are in the organization's best interest (which may be those you either don't do well or are not cost effective for you to do).

Your voices

As far as giving career advice or helping others build their own careers, I encourage folks to challenge themselves and move up the learning curve quickly—to be in your sweet spot after six months on any job. Once an individual has experienced that success—in month seven—I slightly rejigger their responsibilities. At that point, 20 to 30 percent of their job becomes something they're not comfortable with. If it's not painful, you're not growing. And it's that constant, thoughtful reshuffling that helps people in my organization keep growing.[23]

When you have people reporting to you, keep these suggestions in mind:

1. Encourage them to grow as fast as they can.

2. Encourage them to do what they love.

3. Be transparent in your actions and decision-making criteria.

4. Recognize different preferences—a good manager is one who is best attuned to each individual's life lures.

5. Respect their expertise.

6. Give the people you're managing public credit for their accomplishments.

Leading an Organizational Unit

Today, most leadership assignments within an organization last somewhere between two and four years. That's roughly the length of time you'll have to put your mark on how things are done in any one group—to strengthen performance, to shift behavioral norms, and to create a culture that you'll be proud of and enjoy.

The same two considerations that shaped your priorities when delegating to one individual, now broadened to the group you're leading, should determine your overall priorities: what does the business need and what do the people in your organization require. Establish measurable business priorities. Develop a clear vision of how you want people to behave by the end of your tenure.

Because your time in this position is likely to be finite, begin by thinking about the endpoint. What should the announcement of a promotion to your next job say about what you did in this one? Then plan how to achieve these goals in three waves of activity.[24] The goal of the first wave of change should be to secure early wins, build personal credibility, establish key relationships, and identify and harvest low-hanging fruit—the highest-potential opportunities for short-term improvements in organizational performance. This wave, and each to follow, should consist of distinct phases: learning, designing the changes, building support, implementing the changes, and observing results. Done well, this will help you build momentum and deepen your own learning.[25] The second wave of change should address more fundamental issues of strategy, structure, systems, and skills to reshape the organization. This is when the real gains in organizational performance are achieved. Finally, a less extreme wave should focus on fine-tuning to maximize performance. By this point, most leaders are ready to move on to the next challenge.[26]

Whether you take on formal leadership roles or voice your perspectives as senior contributors, I hope you will use your influence to create organizations that are humane and worthy. You deserve to work in places that you respect and feel good about, doing work that you care about. The world needs a new breed of adults, able to acknowledge the complexity and legitimate diversity of views and yet find constructive paths forward. I hope all of you will take heart and find both hope and satisfaction in this challenge.

This is your generation . . . and your time.

NOTES

Note on "Your Voices": Unless otherwise noted, the voices that appear throughout this book are from two sources:

- Responses to my blog posts "10 Reasons Gen Xers Are Unhappy at Work," *Across the Ages*, Harvard Business Online, May 10, 2008 (http://discussionleader.hbsp.com/erickson/2008/05/ten_reasons_why_the_relationsh.html#comments) and "Are There Gender Differences Within Gen X?," *Across the Ages*, Harvard Business Online, May 20, 2008 (http://discussionleader.hbsp.com/erickson/2008/05/are_there_gender_differences_w_1.html#comments):

  Kyle Arteaga, Brian G., Bruce, Chris, Clive Bickerstaff, Dan, Eric, Firehorse, Gattosan, Richard Harrison, Tammy Kobliak, Lance, Laura, LeAnne, Nancy Mehegan, Erinn McMahon, Melissa F., Susan Miller, Diane Murray, Gary Rosenfeld, R. S. Scott, Alyson Silverstein, Daniel Sroka, Michael Temple, Topher, zoby, Laura Zukowski

- Responses to *BusinessWeek*'s feed of "10 Reasons Gen X'ers Are Unhappy at Work," on May 15, 2008, (http://businessweek.com/managing/content/may2008/ca20080515_250308.htm?chan=top+news_top+news+index_news+%2B+analysis):

  Andrew, Earl Barnett III, Carl M, Chelicera, Cheryl, Crystal, D, Dave, David, Bertrand de La Selle, Doug, Dune Girl, Gen Y'er, Geir Gundersen, Gen Xer and Proud, Hopalong, Jay, Jaz, JC, Jessica, Jim, JoeG, John, jonnyd, jz, K, Karl, Charly Leetham, Leo, Markus, Matt, mercenary, Diane Murray, Nora B, Pam, Peter, PurrNaK, Recent Gen-X Refugee, Supriya G., Tara, Thomas, Todd, Tracy, Urban, Gila von Meissner, X as in Ex-employee, Tom Weiss, Where's the love?

Introduction

1. Monci Jo Williams, with H. John Steinbreder, "The Baby Bust Hits the Job Market," *Fortune*, May 27, 1985, 122–135.

2. Christopher Reynolds, "Gen X: The Unbeholden," *American Demographics*, May 1, 2004, http://findarticles.com/p/articles/mi_m4021/is_4_26/ai_n6052824/print.

3. My blog, *Across the Ages*, is available at http://discussionleader.hbsp.com/erickson/.

Chapter One

1. Piaget's theory identifies four developmental stages and the processes by which children progress through them:

1. *Sensorimotor stage (birth–two years old):* The child, through direct physical interaction with his or her environment, builds a set of concepts about reality and how it works. In this stage, a child does not know that physical objects remain in existence even when out of sight. Intelligence takes the form of motor actions.

2. *Preoperational stage (ages two–seven):* The child is not yet able to conceptualize abstractly and needs concrete physical situations. Intelligence is intuitive in nature.

3. *Concrete operations (ages seven–eleven):* As physical experience accumulates, the child starts to conceptualize, creating logical structures that relate to concrete objects or physical experiences. For example, numbers are associated with physical objects and arithmetic equations can be solved.

4. *Formal operations (beginning at ages eleven–fifteen):* By this point, the child's cognitive structures are like those of an adult and include conceptual reasoning. Thinking involves abstractions. Mental models that will persist throughout adulthood are formed.

2. Formative work using the frameworks of child development stages to understand generational patterns includes that done by Morris Massey, "What You Are Is Where You Were When," video program (Cambridge, MA: Enterprise Media, 1986); and William and Neil Howe, *Generations: The History of America's Future, 1584 to 2069* (New York: Quill, William Morrow, 1991).

3. Douglas Coupland, *Generation X: Tales for an Accelerated Culture* (New York: St. Martin's Press, 1991), jacket.

4. William Strauss and Neil Howe, *The Fourth Turning: An American Prophecy*, 1st ed. (New York: Broadway Books, 1997), 210.

5. Strauss and Howe, *Generations: The History of America's Future, 1584 to 2069*, 322.

6. Coupland's original portrait in *Generation X* focused on individuals born between 1961 and 1971.

7. "The Forgotten Generation," a post by Fish Wrap correspondent Black Molly, posted by Phineas F. A. Pickerel, April 22, 2008, http://fishwrap.wordpress.com/2008/04/22/the-forgotten-generation/.

8. Based in part on Allen Floyd Goben, "The X Factor: Generation X Leadership in Early 21st Century American Community Colleges," (PhD dissertation, Graduate School of The University of Texas at Austin, August 2003), 17.

9. Based on Michael R. Muetzel, *They're Not Aloof . . . Just Generation X* (Shreveport, LA: Steel Bay Publishing, 2003), 28.

10. http://www.pbs.org/kcts/videogamerevolution/history/timeline_flash.html.

11. Based on Strauss and Howe, *The Fourth Turning*, 195.

12. Based on ibid.

13. New Strategist Editors, *Generation X: Americans Born 1965 to 1976*, 5th ed., Great American Generations Series (Ithaca, NY: New Strategist Publications, Inc., 2006), 223.

14. Statistics compiled by William Robert Johnston, based on data from the Centers for Disease Control, last updated October 25, 2008, http://www.johnsonsarchive.net/policy/abortion.

15. Geoffrey T. Holtz, *Welcome to the Jungle: The Why Behind Generation X* (New York: St. Martin's Press, 1995), 27.

16. Based on Strauss and Howe, *The Fourth Turning*, 198.

17. Based on Strauss and Howe, *The Fourth Turning*, 197.

18. Interview with Erinn McMahon conducted by author, May 30, 2008.

Chapter Two

1. Monci Jo Williams, with H. John Steinbreder, "The Baby Bust Hits the Job Market," *Fortune*, May 27, 1985, 122–135.

2. Ibid.

3. Douglas Coupland, *Generation X: Tales for an Accelerated Culture* (New York: St. Martin's Press, 1991), 5.

4. Anne Fisher, "Have You Outgrown Your Job?" *Fortune*, August 21, 2006.

5. Personal communication to author.

6. New Strategist Editors, *Generation X: Americans Born 1965 to 1976*, 5th ed., Great American Generations Series (Ithaca, NY: New Strategist Publications, Inc., 2006), 148.

7. Ibid., 154.

8. Ibid., 162.

9. Findings from the research project, the Families and Work Institute National Study of the Changing Workforce, conducted in 2002 with a sample size of approximately 3,500 wage and salaried employees and self-employed workers, cited in "Generation and Gender in the Workplace" (Watertown, MA: Families and Work Institute, American Business Collaboration, 2004), 5.

10. Lawrence E. Gladieux and Arthur M. Hauptman, *The College Aid Quandary: Access, Quality, and the Federal Role* (Washington, DC: The Brookings Institution, 1995).

11. Government Accountability Office data, cited in New Strategist Editors, *Generation X*, 298.

12. Kleber & Associates, "Lingering Myths about Generation X: Dispelling Myths About the 'Lost' Generation," housingzone.com, February 1, 2005, http://www.housingzone.com/article/CA503868.html.

13. New Strategist Editors, *Generation X*, 84.

14. Ibid., 94.

15. Ibid., 298.

16. Research conducted by Dwight Burlingame, associate executive director of Indiana University's Center on Philanthropy, based on GAO data, as quoted in Kimberly Palmer,

"Gen X-ers: Stingy or Strapped?" *Money and Business*, http://www.usnews.com/usnews/biztech/articles/070214/14genX'ers.htm.

17. New Strategist Editors, *Generation X*, 298.

18. Carrie Lips, "Gen X Finding Its Voice," *Jacksonville Journal-Courier*, December 29, 1998, citing research by the Cato Institute, http://www.socialsecurity.org/pubs/articles/cl-12-29-98.html.

19. Cayman Seacrest, "Study, Gen X," University of Colorado, 1996, http://www.cc.colorado.edu/Dept/EC/generationx96/genx.

20. New Strategist Editors, *Generation X*, 54.

21. Marisa DiNatale and Stephanie Boraas, "The Labor Force Experience of Women from 'Generation X,'" *Monthly Labor Review*, Bureau of Labor Statistics, 2002.

22. For example, in Canada, the median for men is thirty-four and for women, thirty-three. In France, the median age is thirty-seven for men and twenty-nine for women; in Sweden, thirty-three for men and thirty-one for women; and in the United Kingdom, thirty for men and twenty-eight for women. For more information, see Jeffrey Jensen Arnett, *Emerging Adulthood: The Winding Road from the Late Teens Through the Twenties* (New York, Oxford: Oxford University Press, 2004).

23. DiNatale and Boraas, "The Labor Force Experience, 2002." (Comparable data for men is not available.)

24. Ibid.

25. "Generation X is in no hurry to settle down," says Ethan Watters, who charts their social meandering in James Sullivan, "Urban Tribes," *San Francisco Chronicle*, October 10, 2003, http://sfgate.com/cgi-bin/article.cgi?f=/c/a/2003/10/10/DD203007.DTL. See also Ethan Watters, *Urban Tribes: Are Friends the New Family?* (London: Bloomsbury, 2003), 8.

26. Interview of Esteban Herrera conducted by author, May 30, 2008.

27. Robert D. Putnam, *Bowling Alone: The Collapse and Revival of American Community* (New York: Simon & Schuster, 2000), 287.

28. Personal communication from Esteban Herrera to author, August 22, 2008.

29. Bruce J. Klein, "This Wonderful Lengthening of Lifespan," *The Longevity Meme*, January 17, 2003, http://www.longevitymeme.org/articles.

30. E. Fussell and F. Furstenberg, "The Transition to Adulthood During the 20th Century: Race, Nativity and Gender," Network on Transitions to Adulthood (Philadelphia, PA, 2004; funded by the MacArthur Foundation).

31. Cheryl Merser, *Grown-ups: A Generation in Search of Adulthood* (New York: Putnam, 1987); cited in James Cote, *Arrested Adulthood: The Changing Nature of Maturity and Identity* (New York and London: New York University Press, 2000), 14–15.

32. Cote, *Arrested Adulthood*.

33. Personal communication from Joe Grochowski to author, October 2, 2007.

34. As quoted by Thomas L. Friedman, "Opinion: Kicking Over the Chessboard," *New York Times*, April 18, 2004.

35. Robert Kegan, *The Evolving Self: Problem and Process in Human Development* (Cambridge, MA, and London: Harvard University Press, 1982), 11.

36. Ibid., 120

37. Cote, *Arrested Adulthood*, 14–15.

Chapter Three

1. In general, generational experiences become more similar as we consider younger cohorts. Older generations exhibit significant country-by-country variation, since the environments in individual countries were often substantially different.

2. 1974 Gallup poll quoted in "The Good-News Generation," *U.S. News & World Report*, November 3, 2003, 60.

3. Jeff Gordinier, *X Saves the World: How Generation X Got the Shaft but Can Still Keep Everything from Sucking* (New York: Viking Penguin, 2008), 101.

4. Quoted in Gordinier, *X Saves the World*, 71.

5. Ibid., 69.

6. David Brooks, "The Odyssey Years," *New York Times*, October 9, 2007.

7. Louise Story, "Many Women at Elite Colleges Set Career Path to Motherhood," *New York Times*, September 20, 2005.

8. Gordinier, *X Saves the World*, 69–70.

Chapter Four

1. Personal communication to author from Jason Siedel.

2. "The Forgotten Generation," a post by Fish Wrap correspondent Black Molly, posted by Phineas F. A. Pickerel, April 22, 2008, http://fishwrap.wordpress.com/2008/04/22/the-forgotten-generation/.

3. The Concours Group (now nGenera) and Age Wave, "The New Employee/Employer Equation," 2004. This research project included a nationwide survey of over seventy-seven hundred employees conducted in June 2004 by Harris Interactive for The Concours Group (now nGenera) and Age Wave.

4. Catalyst, "The Next Generation: Today's Professionals, Tomorrow's Leaders," December 11, 2001. A survey conducted of over twelve hundred professionals born between 1964 and 1975 from eight companies in the United States and two in Canada.

5. The Families and Work Institute/American Business Collaboration, "Generation and Gender in the Workplace," 2004, 25. Cites findings from the research project, "The Families and Work Institute National Study of the Changing Workforce," conducted in 2002 with a sample size of approximately thirty-five hundred wage and salaried employees and self-employed workers.

6. Toddi Gutner, "A Balancing Act for Gen X Women," BusinessWeek Online, January 21, 2002, http://www.businessweek.com/magazine/content/02_03/b3766112.htm, reporting on a study of thirteen hundred professionals aged twenty-six to thirty-seven, skewed toward women (representing 70 percent of the respondents).

7. Margot Hornblower, "Great Xpectations of So-Called Slackers," TIME.com, June 9, 1997, http://www.time.com/time/magazine/article/0,9171,986481,00.html.

8. Jeff Gordinier, *X Saves the World: How Generation X Got the Shaft but Can Still Keep Everything from Sucking* (New York: Viking Penguin, 2008), 50.

9. Karen S. Peterson, "Gen X Moms Have It Their Way," *USA Today*, May 14, 2003.

10. Marisa DiNatale and Stephanie Boraas, "The Labor Force Experience of Women from 'Generation X,'" *Monthly Labor Review*, Bureau of Labor Statistics, 2002.

11. Jamie-Andrea Yanak, "Gen X Parents Sharing More with Kids," Associated Press, April 5, 2006.

12. Patricia Wen, "Gen X Dad," *Boston Globe*, January 16, 2005.

13. Peterson, "Gen X Moms Have It Their Way."

14. Ibid.

15. Douglas Coupland, *Generation X: Tales for an Accelerated Culture* (New York: St. Martin's Press, 1991), 54.

16. Gordinier, *X Saves the World*, 126.

17. Kleber & Associates, "Lingering Myths About Generation X: Dispelling Myths About the 'Lost' Generation," housingzone.com, February 1, 2005, http://www.housingzone.com/article/CA503868.html.

18. Gutner, "A Balancing Act for Gen X Women."

19. Wen, "Gen X Dad."

20. Personal communication to author from HH.

21. Gutner, "A Balancing Act for Gen X Women."

22. Sylvia Ann Hewlett, *Off-Ramps and On-Ramps: Keeping Talented Women on the Road to Success* (Boston: Harvard Business School Press, 2007).

23. Gutner, "A Balancing Act for Gen X Women."

24. AD Staff, "Farther ALONG the X Axis," *American Demographics*, May 1, 2004, http://findarticles.com/p/articles/mi_m4021/is_4_26/ai_n6080026.

25. Ann A. Fishman, president of Generational-Targeted Marketing Corp., New Orleans, quoted in ibid.

26. Daniel H. Pink, *The Adventures of Johnny Bunko: The Last Career Guide You'll Ever Need* (New York: Riverhead Books, 2008).

27. Tom Rath and Donald Clifton, "The Power of Praise and Recognition," *Gallup Management Journal*, July 8, 2004.

28. Based on the work of Jeffrey Pfeffer, professor of Organizational Behavior in the Graduate School of Business at Stanford University, as incorporated in Re.sult Project EMP, *Excelling at Employee Engagement*, The Concours Group (now nGenera), 2005.

29. Robert Morison, Tamara J. Erickson, and Ken Dychtwald, "Managing Middlescence," *Harvard Business Review*, March 2006, 78–86.

30. A 2005 Conference Board survey cited in Morison, Erickson, and Dychtwald, "Managing Middlescence."

31. Ibid.

32. Pink, *The Adventures of Johnny Bunko*.

33. The notion of *flow* is a concept developed by Mihaly Csikszentmihalyi, professor of psychology and management, Drucker School of Management, Claremont Graduate University. See, for example, Mihaly Csikszentmihalyi, *Finding Flow: The Psychology of Engagement with Everyday Life* (New York: Basic Books, 1997).

34. Elizabeth Debold, "Flow with Soul: An Interview with Dr. Mihaly Csikszentmihalyi," *What Is Enlightenment?* (Spring/Summer 2002), http://www.enlightennext.org/magazine/j21/csiksz.asp.

35. Csikszentmihalyi, *Finding Flow*.

36. Based on the work of Jim Loehr, founder of LGE Performance Systems. See Jim Loehr and Tony Schwartz, *The Power of Full Engagement: Managing Energy, not Time, Is the Key to High Performance and Personal Renewal* (New York: Free Press, 2003).

37. Concours Group (now nGenera) and Age Wave, "The New Employee/Employer Equation."

38. Ibid.

39. For more on engagement, see Tamara J. Erickson and Lynda Gratton, "What It Means to Work Here," *Harvard Business Review*, March 2007, 104–112.

Chapter Five

1. "Meeting the Challenges of Tomorrow's Workplace," *Chief Executive*, August–September 2002.

2. Ibid.

3. Deepak Ramachandran and Paul Artiuch, "Harnessing the Global N-Gen Talent Pool" (Toronto: New Paradigm Learning Corporation, 2007).

4. New Strategist Editors, *Generation X: Americans Born 1965 to 1976*, 5th ed., Great American Generations Series (Ithaca, NY: New Strategist Publications, Inc., 2006), 226.

5. Ibid., 229.

6. Brian Whitley, "With Fewer Jobs, Fewer Illegal Immigrants," *Christian Science Monitor*, December 30, 2008.

7. "The Battle for Brainpower," *The Economist*, October 5, 2006, www.economist.com/surveys/displayStory.cfm?story_id=7961894.

8. Jeff Gordinier, *X Saves the World: How Generation X Got the Shaft but Can Still Keep Everything from Sucking* (New York: Viking Penguin, 2008), 114.

9. Harold Adams Innis, *The Bias of Communication* (Toronto: University of Toronto Press, 1964).

10. See Umair Haque's blog "Edge Economy," Harvard Business Online, http://discussionleader.hbsp.com/haque/.

11. See Bill Taylor's blog "Practically Radical," Harvard Business Online, http://blogs.harvardbusiness.org/taylor/.

12. Don Tapscott and Anthony D. Williams, *Wikinomics: How Mass Collaboration Changes Everything* (London: Portfolio, 2006), 269.

13. Ibid.

14. Umair Haque, "Edge Economy."

15. Ibid.

16. Tapscott and Williams, *Wikinomics*, 269.

17. For a more extensive discussion of the formation of "hot spots," see Lynda Gratton, *Hot Spots: Why Some Teams, Workplaces, and Organizations Buzz with Energy—and Others Don't* (San Francisco: Berrett-Koehler, 2007).

18. Ricardo Semler, *The Seven-Day Weekend: Changing the Way Work Works* (New York: Portfolio, 2004), 114.

19. Haque, "Edge Economy."

20. Jason Fried, CEO of 37signals, and his colleague David Heinemeier Hansson, creator of the much-celebrated Ruby on Rails programming framework, as cited by Bill Taylor, "Practically Radical."

21. Semler, *The Seven-Day Weekend*.

22. Taylor, "Practically Radical."

23. Sylvia Ann Hewlett and Carolyn Buck Luce, "Off-Ramps and On-Ramps: Keeping Talented Women on the Road to Success," *Harvard Business Review*, March 2005, 43–54.

24. The Concours Group (now nGenera) and Age Wave, "The New Employee/ Employer Equation," 2004. This research project included a nationwide survey of over seventy-seven hundred employees conducted in June 2004 by Harris Interactive for The Concours Group (now nGenera) and Age Wave.

25. Ibid.

26. Barbara Rose, "Workers Selecting Own Career Track," *Chicago Tribune*, September 9, 2007, chicagotribune.com. For further information, see Cathleen Benko and Anne Weisberg, *Mass Career Customization: Aligning the Workplace with Today's Nontraditional Workforce* (Boston: Harvard Business School Press, 2007).

27. Semler, *The Seven-Day Weekend*, 52.

28. Bill Taylor, "Practically Radical."

29. Ken Dychtwald, Tamara J. Erickson, and Robert Morison, *Workforce Crisis: How to Avoid the Coming Shortage of Skills and Talent* (Boston: Harvard Business School Press, 2006).

30. Haque, "Edge Economy."

31. Ibid.

32. Stefanie Sanford and Steven Seleznow, "Generational Change: Some Controversial Cause for Optimism in Educational Policy," Harvard Law and Policy Review Online, http://www.hlpronline.com/2007/04/seleznow_sanford_01.html.

33. Barack Obama, "21st Century Schools for a 21st Century Economy," speech delivered March 13, 2006.

34. Sanford and Seleznow, "Generational Change."

35. Ibid.

36. Ibid.

37. Harry J. Holzer and Robert I. Lerman, "American's Forgotten Middle-Skill Jobs," (Washington, DC: The Workforce Alliance, November 2007).

38. Personal communication to author from Dark Past, May 20, 2008.

39. The Council for Excellence in Government and The Gallup Organization, "Within Reach . . . But Out of Synch: The Possibilities and Challenges of Shaping Tomorrow's Government Workforce," December 5, 2006.

40. Thomas L. Friedman, *The World Is Flat: A Brief History of the Twenty-first Century* (New York: Farrar, Straus and Giroux, 2006), 240–243.

Chapter Six

1. New Strategist Editors, *Generation X: Americans Born 1965 to 1976*, 5th ed., Great American Generations Series (Ithaca, NY: New Strategist Publications, Inc., 2006), 165.

2. www.myersbriggs.org.

3. For more information, see wikipedia.org/wiki/Lateralization_of_brain_function.

4. www.strengthsfinder.com.

5. www.rypple.com.

6. Based on Peter Scott-Morgan's *The Unwritten Rules of the Game: Master Them, Shatter Them, and Break Through the Barriers to Organizational Change* (New York: McGraw-Hill, 1994); and Hidden Logic Imperative, a research report by The Concours Group (now nGenera), January 1, 2005.

7. Joseph Grenny, David Maxfield, and Andrew Shimberg, "How to Have Influence," *MIT Sloan Management Review*, Fall 2008, 47–52.

8. See, for example, Stephen R. Covey, *The Seven Habits of Highly Effective People* (New York: Free Press, 2004).

9. Based on Robert Morison, Tamara J. Erickson, and Ken Dychtwald, "Managing Middlescence," *Harvard Business Review*, March 2006, 78–86.

10. Based on ibid.

11. Based on Ricardo Semler, *The Seven-Day Weekend: Changing the Way Work Works* (New York: Portfolio, 2004), 146–147.

12. Morison, Erickson, and Dychtwald, "Managing Middlescence."

13. Ibid., citing the research report by The Concours Group (now nGenera) and Age Wave, "The New Employee/Employer Equation," 2004.

14. Lynne C. Lancaster and David Stillman, *When Generations Collide* (New York: Harper Collins, 2002), 207.

15. Based on William Strauss and Neil Howe, *The Fourth Turning: An American Prophecy* (New York: Broadway Books, 1997), 241.

16. Michael R. Muetzel, *They're Not Aloof . . . Just Generation X* (Shreveport, LA: Steel Bay Publishing, 2003), 23–24.

17. Based in part on Allen Floyd Goben, "The X Factor: Generation X Leadership in Early 21st Century American Community Colleges" (PhD dissertation, University of Texas at Austin, 2003), 1–2.

18. Based in part on ibid.

19. "Managing a Job Change," Heritage Planning, 2000, www.lktax.com/pdf_docs/email/ls/5/0008.pdf.

20. Based on Strauss and Howe, *The Fourth Turning*, 241.

21. Interview with Beth Hilbing conducted by author, June 16, 2008.

22. New Strategist Editors, *Generation X: Americans Born 1965 to 1976*, 12–15.

23. Ibid.

24. Ibid., 24.

25. Ibid., 129.

26. Interview of Rory Madden conducted by author, May 14, 2008.

27. Interview of Eric Kimble conducted by author, October 9, 2007.

28. Mark Granovetter, "The Strength of Weak Ties," *American Journal of Sociology* 78, no. 6 (May 1973): 1360–1380.

29. Lynda Gratton, *Hot Spots: Why Some Teams, Workplaces, and Organizations Buzz with Energy—and Others Don't* (San Francisco: Berrett-Koehler, 2007), 72.

30. James Sullivan, "Generation X Is In No Hurry To Settle Down, Says Ethan Watters," *San Francisco Chronicle*, October 10, 2003, http://sfgate.com/cgi-bin/article.cgi?f=/c/a/2003/10/10/DD203007.DTL.

31. Based on ibid.

32. Ethan Watters, *Urban Tribes: Are Friends the New Family?* (New York: Bloomsbury, 2003), 107.

33. Ibid., 113.

34. Interview of Mike Dover conducted by author, May 28, 2008.

35. Speech at an executive summit, The Concours Group, March 30, 1999, Pebble Beach, Monterey, CA.

36. Nadira A. Hira, "My X'er Boss Hates Me!," *Fortune*, September 28, 2007, http://thegig.blogs.fortune.com/.

37. Interview of Esteban Herrera conducted by author, May 30, 2008.

38. Lionel Bart, *Oliver!*

Chapter Seven

1. Interview of Steven Kramer by author, October 9, 2007.

2. Personal communication from David Jenkins to author, May 20, 2008.

3. Posted by John Jacobs, November 19, 2006, 9:43 p.m., Fortune TalkBack, "Call it the Gray Ceiling," http://talkback.blogs.fortune.com/2006/8/10/the-big-difficult/.

4. Based on a survey conducted by Encino, CA–based E-Poll of 1,032 online respondents, as quoted in Christopher Reynolds, "Gen X: The Unbeholden," *American Demographics*, May 2004, http://findarticles.com/p/articles/mi_m4021/is_4_26/ai_n6052824/print. The sample skewed slightly male and higher income than the general population, but respondents' age and race closely matches census estimates.

5. New Strategist Editors, *Generation X: Americans Born 1965 to 1976*, 5th ed., Great American Generations Series (Ithaca, NY: New Strategist Publications, Inc., 2006), 170.

6. Reynolds, "Gen X: The Unbeholden."

7. Interview of Esteban Herrera, conducted by author on May 30, 2008. Within several months of this interview, Esteban had resigned from his corporate job and set out to form his own company.

8. Pew Research Center poll of 2,003 Americans ages eighteen and over, cited in Sharon Jayson, "Gen Y Makes a Mark and Their Imprint Is Entrepreneurship," *USA Today*, December 12, 2006.

9. Thomas W. Malone, *The Future of Work: How the New Order of Business Will Shape Your Organization, Your Management Style, and Your Life* (Boston: Harvard Business School Press, 2004).

10. Kramer, interview.

11. William D. Bygrave, "The Entrepreneurial Process," in *The Portable MBA in Entrepreneurship*, 3rd ed., eds. William D. Bygrave and Andrew Zacharaki (Hoboken, NJ: John Wiley & Sons, 2004), 4. Bygrave quotes a 2002 study of the *Inc.* 500.

12. Interview of Rebecca Minard by author, November 2, 2007.

13. Kramer, interview.

14. Key points, as well as the suggested readings included in footnotes 15–19 and 21–23, are drawn from James M. Manyika, Roger P. Roberts, and Kara L. Sprague, "Eight Business Technology Trends to Watch," *McKinsey Quarterly*, December 2007.

15. For further reading: Bradford C. Johnson, James M. Manyika, and Lareina A. Yee, "The Next Revolution in Interactions," November 2005, mckinseyquarterly.com; Scott C. Beardsley, Bradford C. Johnson, and James M. Manyika, "Competitive Advantage from Better Interactions," May 2006, mckinseyquarterly.com; Malone, *The Future of Work*.

16. For further reading: John Hagel III, *Out of the Box: Strategies for Achieving Profits Today and Growth Tomorrow Through Web Services* (Boston: Harvard Business School Press, 2002); Claus Heinrich, *RFID and Beyond: Growing Your Business with Real World Awareness* (Indianapolis, IN: Wiley Publishing, 2005); Jeanne W. Ross, Peter Weill, and David C. Robertson, *Enterprise Architecture as Strategy: Creating a Foundation for Business Execution* (Boston: Harvard Business School Press, 2006).

17. For further reading: Thomas H. Davenport and Jeanne G. Harris, *Competing on Analytics: The New Science of Winning* (Boston: Harvard Business School Press, 2007); John Riedl and Joseph Konstan, with Eric Vrooman, *Word of Mouse: The Marketing Power of Collaborative Filtering* (New York: Warner Books, 2002); Stefan H. Thomke, *Experimentation Matters: Unlocking the Potential of New Technologies for Innovation*, (Boston: Harvard Business School Press, 2003); David Weinberger, *Everything Is Miscellaneous: The Power of the New Digital Disorder* (New York: Times Books, 2007).

18. For further reading: Carl Shapiro and Hal R. Varian, *Information Rules: A Strategic Guide to the Network Economy* (Boston: Harvard Business School Press, 1999).

19. For further reading: Hal R. Varian, Joseph Farrell, and Carl Shapiro, *The Economics of Information Technology: An Introduction (Raffaele Mattioli Lectures)* (New York: Cambridge University Press, 2004).

20. Minard, interview.

21. For further reading: Yochai Benkler, *The Wealth of Networks: How Social Production Transforms Markets and Freedom* (New Haven, CT: Yale University Press, 2006); Henry Chesbrough, *Open Innovation: The New Imperative for Creating and Profiting from Technology* (Boston: Harvard Business School Press, 2003); James Surowiecki, *The Wisdom of Crowds: Why the Many Are Smarter than the Few and How Collective Wisdom Shapes Business, Economies, Societies, and Nations* (New York: Doubleday, 2004); Eric von Hippel, *Democratizing Innovation* (Cambridge, MA: MIT Press, 2005).

22. For further reading: Richard Florida, *The Rise of the Creative Class: And How It's Transforming Work, Leisure, Community, and Everyday Life* (New York: Basic Books, 2004); Daniel H. Pink, *Free Agent Nation: How America's New Independent Workers Are Transforming the Way We Live* (New York: Warner Books, 2001).

23. For further reading: C. K. Prahalad and Venkat Ramaswamy, *The Future of Competition: Co-Creating Unique Value with Customers* (Boston: Harvard Business School Press, 2004); Don Tapscott and Anthony D. Williams, *Wikinomics: How Mass Collaboration Changes Everything* (New York: Portfolio Hardcover, 2006).

24. "How Businesses Are Using Web 2.0: A McKinsey Global Survey," March 2007, mckinseyquarterly.com.

25. For further reading: "Jeff Bezos' Risky Bet," *BusinessWeek*, November 13, 2006.

26. Kramer, interview.
27. Ibid.
28. Ibid.
29. Minard, interview.
30. Ibid.
31. Kramer, interview.
32. Minard, interview.
33. Kramer, interview.
34. Personal communications from Jean Ayers to author, September 12, 2007, and September 21, 2008.
35. Ibid.
36. Hazel Markus and Paula Nurius, "Possible Selves," *American Psychologist* 41, no. 9 (1986): 954–969, quoted in Herminia Ibarra, *Working Identity: Unconventional Strategies for Reinventing Your Career* (Boston: Harvard Business School Press, 2003), 13.
37. Ibarra, *Working Identity*, 35.
38. Tamara Erickson, *Retire Retirement: Career Strategies for the Boomer Generation* (Boston: Harvard Business Press, 2008).
39. Richard T. Pascale, Mark Milleman, and Linda Gioja, *Surfing the Edge of Chaos: The Laws of Nature and the New Laws of Business* (New York: Crown Business, 2000).
40. Ibarra, *Working Identity*, xi.

Chapter Eight

1. William Strauss and Neil Howe, *Generations: The History of America's Future, 1584 to 2069* (New York: Quill, William Morrow, 1991), 317–334.
2. Based on Stefanie Sanford and Steven Seleznow, "Generational Change: Some Controversial Cause for Optimism in Educational Policy," Harvard Law and Policy Review Online, Official Journal of the American Constitution Society for Law and Policy; http://www.hlpronline.com/2007/04/seleznow_sanford_01.html.
3. Based on Sanford and Seleznow.
4. William Strauss and Neil Howe, *The Fourth Turning: An American Prophecy*, 1st ed. (New York: Broadway Books, 1997), 326.
5. Cameron Sinclair, cofounder of Architecture for Humanity, quoted in Jeff Gordinier, *X Saves the World: How Generation X Got the Shaft but Can Still Keep Everything from Sucking* (New York: Viking Penguin, 2008), 151.
6. Quoted in ibid., 129.
7. Personal communication with Lynda Gratton based on her research, Lehman Centre for Women in Business.
8. Gordinier, *X Saves the World*, 169–170.
9. *Roget's 21st Century Thesaurus*, 3rd ed., copyright 2008 by the Philip Lief Group, retrieved from website: http://dictionary.reference.com/browse/leadership.
10. Ronald Heifetz, *Leadership Without Easy Answers* (Cambridge, MA: Harvard University Press, 1998).

11. R. A. Heifetz and R. M. Sinder, "Political Leadership: Managing the Public's Problem Solving," in *The Power of Public Ideas*, ed. R. Reich (Cambridge, MA: Harvard University Press, 1990), 179–203.

12. Research conducted with Lynda Gratton and a team at London Business School in 2006.

13. For further information on the research and a more detailed description of our findings, see Lynda Gratton, Andreas Voigt, and Tamara J. Erickson, "Bridging Faultlines in Diverse Teams," *MIT Sloan Management Review*, Summer 2007, 22–29; and Lynda Gratton and Tamara J. Erickson, "Eight Ways to Build Collaborative Teams," *Harvard Business Review*, November 2007, 100–109.

14. You can map the frequency of information exchange among individuals using tools such as the one developed by Robert Cross at the University of Virginia, creating rich visual representations of the relationships of collaboration within an organization and, conversely, identifying those parts of the organization where little exchange occurs. For further information, see Robert Cross and Andrew Parker, *The Hidden Power of Social Networks: Understanding How Work Really Gets Done in Organizations* (Boston: Harvard Business School Press, 2004).

15. Ricardo Semler, *The Seven-Day Weekend: Changing the Way Work Works* (New York: Portfolio, 2004), 166.

16. Ibid., 118.

17. John F. Kennedy, speech, Rice University, September 12, 1962.

18. For further information, see Richard T. Pascale, Mark Milleman, and Linda Gioja, *Surfing the Edge of Chaos: The Laws of Nature and the New Laws of Business* (New York: Crown Business, 2000).

19. Heifetz, *Leadership Without Easy Answers*.

20. Interview of Rebecca Minard conducted by author, November 2, 2007.

21. Ibid.

22. Michael R. Muetzel, *They're Not Aloof . . . Just Generation X* (Shreveport, LA: Steel Bay Publishing, 2003), 30.

23. Eric Kimble, interview with author, October 9, 2007.

24. John J. Gabarro, *The Dynamics of Taking Charge* (Boston: Harvard Business School Press, 1987).

25. Michael Watkins, *The First 90 Days: Critical Success Strategies for New Leaders at All Levels* (Boston: Harvard Business School Press, 2003).

26. For additional advice, particularly about beginning a new leadership assignment, see Watkins, *The First 90 Days*.

INDEX

abortion rates, 16
AIDS, 16
Allen, Paul, 11
alternative rock, 13
alternative workplaces
  back-up jobs, 182–183
  desire for security and self-reliance, 163–165
  entrepreneurship (*see* entrepreneurship)
  work arrangements/contracting, 167–170
  X'ers motivation to move into, 165–166
Arrested Adulthood (Cote), 42
availability of work. *See* employment and the economy
Ayers, Jean, 180–181

Beck, 13
The Bias of Communication (Innis), 105
birth rates worldwide, 98–99
Boomers
  approach to sharing information, 207
  approach to team work, 207
  competitiveness, 50–51
  conflicts with Gen X'ers, 51–53
  demographics, 49
  managing, 210–212
  relationship with Gen X'ers, 24–26, 143–145
  relationship with their children, 67–68
  retirements, 99
  teen years, 49
  view of winning, 43–44
  world events during lifetime, 50
boundary spanner, 146
Bowling Alone (Putnam), 34
Bright Horizons, 88
Brooks, David, 56
Burnt Generation, 8

career strategies
  breadth of experience goal, 152–154
  education to expand options, 151
  entrepreneurship (*see* entrepreneurship)
  exploring and experimenting, 184–185
  increasing your effectiveness at work (*see* effectiveness at work)
  job-hopping as a value-adding strategy, 147–150
  networking, 155–156
  new work arrangements/contracting, 167–170
  portfolio careers/back-up jobs, 182–184
  taking the initiative ideas, 146–147
  work/life balance considerations, 157–162
Challenger incident, 10–11
choice economy, 105–106
Civil Rights Act (1964), 15
Cobain, Kurt, 13
Colbert, Stephen, 36
Cold War, 9
computers and the Internet, 11–12

Index

The Container Store, 89
Cote, James, 38, 42
Coupland, Douglas, 4, 6, 71
Crisis Generation, 8

demographics
  abortion rates, 16
  age of marriage and children, 31
  birth rates worldwide, 98–99
  Boomers, 49
  divorce rates, 16
  Generation X, 6–8
  Generation Y, 53
  growth rate of working-age populations, 101, 102
  household income, 27
  immigration and, 100–101
  job patterns, 104
  labor force composition shifts, 45
  long-term demand for labor, 101
  Re-Generation, 57
  Traditionalists, 45
  unemployment in 1980s and 90s, 22–23
  women in the workforce, 68–70, 73–74
Dover, Mike, 155–156
Dungeons and Dragons, 12

early adult years
  college-related debt, 27–28
  dot-com bust impact, 30–31
  emphasis on self-reliance, 41
  financial commitments, 29–30
  friendships importance, 32–35
  home ownership costs, 28–29
  household income, 27
  job market challenges, 22–24
  life expectancy, 36–37
  marriage and children, 31
  net worth drop, 29
  relationship with Boomers, 24–26
  relationship with Gen Y's, 25–26
  sense of humor, 35–36
  shift in milestones, 37–39
  stages of adulthood and, 41–42
  transition to adulthood, 38
  view of careers and life, 39–40
edge economy, 106
education in a career strategy, 151
effectiveness at work
  building more constructive relationships, 145
  calibration of career potential issue, 127–128
  career strategies (*see* career strategies)
  creating the context for success, 133–135
  evolving sense of self issue, 127
  influencing the organization, 135–136
  keeping up and prioritizing, 138–140
  leveraging corporate benefits, 141–142
  leveraging your track record, 142
  managing up, 143–145
  playing to your strengths, 129–133
  shifting roles issue, 126–127
  understanding each role you play, 136–138
employment and the economy
  birth rates worldwide and, 98–99
  Boomer retirements, 99
  college related debt, 27–28
  dot-com bust impact, 30–31
  financial commitments, 29–30
  during Gen X'ers teen years, 8–9
  home ownership costs, 28–29
  household income, 27
  immigration and, 100–101
  job market challenges, 22–24
  near-term economy and, 101, 103
  net worth drop, 29
  outsourcing, 99–100
  productivity and, 101
engagement at work
  energy of engagement, 80–81
  experience of flow, 79–80
  what engages you worksheet, 85–86
  work engagement quiz, 78–79

entrepreneurship
- develop a good plan, 175–178
- embrace a good idea, 172–175
- find the right skills and money, 178–179
- Gen X'ers desire for, 170–171, 180–182
- network and get advice, 179–180
- odds for and against, 171–172

Equal Rights Amendment (ERA), 15
Esteban's story, 32–34
The Evolving Self: Problem and Process in Human Development (Kegan), 41
expressive legacy archetype, 87–88
ExxonMobil, 89

Ferraro, Geraldine, 15
Ferren, Bran, 157
flexible support archetype, 92–94
flow and engagement at work, 79–80
The Fourth Turning (Strauss and Howe), 4, 143
Fried, Jason, 111
Friedman, Thomas, 123

Gates, Bill, 11
gay rights movement, 16
Génération Bof, 8
Generations (Strauss and Howe), 4, 188
Generation X
- approach to sharing information, 207
- approach to team work, 207
- common traits, 4–6
- common values, 63
- current life issues (*see* early adult years)
- demographics, 6–8
- desires shared by members (*see* shared desires of X'ers)
- managing, 212–213
- relationship with Boomers, 24–26, 44, 51–53, 143–145
- relationship with Gen Y's, 25–26, 57
- teen years (*see* teen years)
- useful traits, 5–6
- voices of (*see* voices of Gen X)

Generation X: Tales for an Accelerated Culture (Coupland), 4
Generation Y
- approach to work, 207
- demographics, 53
- feedback and, 208
- leading, 208–210
- level of parental attention received, 54–55
- relationship with Gen X'ers, 25–26, 57
- technology and, 56
- world events during lifetime, 54

Gioja, Linda, 185
Gisholt, Paal, 173, 179
Gratton, Lynda, 155
Greer, Bill, 123
Grown-ups: A Generation in Search of Adulthood (Merser), 38

Haley, Alex, 15
Haque, Umair, 106, 110
Havel, Václav, 189
Heifetz, Ronald, 192
Hewett, Sylvia Ann, 114
Hibling, Beth, 148
Hofer, Barbara, 55
Howe, Neil, 4, 18, 19, 55, 143, 148, 188, 189

Ibarra, Herminia, 184
ideagoras, 107
immigration and job availability, 100–101
individual desires search
- elements of career satisfaction, 76
- energy of engagement, 80–81
- experience of flow, 79–80
- middlescence dilemma, 77–78
- personal life lures (*see* personal life lures)
- personal nature of the quest, 75
- work engagement quiz, 78–79

individual expertise archetype, 90–91

Innis, Harold Adams, 105, 106
the Internet, 11–12

JetBlue, 94
Joe's story, 39–40

Kegan, Robert, 41, 42
Kimble, Eric, 153
Kopp, Wendy, 120

Lancaster, Lynne, 143
latchkey kids, 16
leadership by Gen X'ers
  asking compelling questions, 197–198
  best practices use, 204–205
  challenges being faced, 187–188
  collaborative environment establishment, 195–197
  complexity and disruptive information and, 198–199
  concept of vision and, 199–200
  context-creating responsibilities, overview, 193
  current leadership norms, 191
  diversity and, 205–206
  employees' values and preferences and, 201–202
  gaps in perceptions between groups, 206–208
  idealism traded for realism, 188–189
  innovation definition, 194
  leading Gen Y, 208–210
  managing Boomers, 210–212
  managing other Gen X'ers, 212–213
  need for new approaches, 192
  one-on-one, 214–215
  opportunity to change corporate template, 189
  of organizational units, 215–216
  organization's distinctive characteristics, showcasing, 202–204
  organization's values identification, 200–201
  relationship's importance, 194
  signature experience development, 203
limited obligations archetype, 94–95
Linklater, Richard, 6
Luce, Caroline Buck, 114

Madden, Rory, 153
Malone, Thomas W., 171
Merser, Cheryl, 38
middlescence dilemma, 77–78
Milleman, Mark, 185
Millennial Generation. *See* Generation Y
Minard, Becky, 173, 179
Moral Majority, 16
MTV, 12, 13
Muetzel, Michel, 144, 213

nature of work
  changes in forms of value creation, 105
  considerations for a future job, 123
  drivers of changes in, 104–105
  education options, 120
  government service and the military, 122
  job patterns, 104
  nonprofits and social entrepreneurship, 120
  opportunities for job growth, 118–119
  professional services, 119–120
  trades and middle-skill jobs, 121
near-term economy and job availability, 101, 103
networking in a career strategy, 155–156
New Leaders for New Schools, 120
New Teacher Project (NTP), 120
Nirvana, 13
Nokia, 196

Obama, Barack, 6
OhMyNews, 176
organizations
  best practices use, 204–205
  concept of vision and, 199–200
  current characteristics of, 108
  distinctive characteristics, showcasing, 202–204
  employees' values and preferences and, 201–202
  evolving characteristics of, 107–108
  key changes expected, 111–118
  leadership of organizational units, 215–216
  new assumptions, 110
  old assumptions, 108–110
  opportunity to change corporate template, 189
  signature experience development, 203
  values identification, 200–201
outsourcing and job availability, 99–100

Pascale, Richard, 185
personal life lures
  archetypes overview, 82–84
  categorizing situations, 82, 83
  expressive legacy archetype, 87–88
  flexible support archetype, 92–94
  individual expertise and team victory archetype, 90–91
  individual expertise archetype, 90–91
  limited obligations archetype, 94–95
  risk with reward archetype, 91–92
  secure progress archetype, 88–90
  team victory archetype, 90–91
  what engages you worksheet, 85–86
Piaget, Jean, 3
portfolio careers/back-up jobs, 182–184
productivity and job availability, 101
Putnam, Robert, 34

Radiohead, 13
Re-Generation, 57–59
reproductive choice, 16
Rhee, Michelle, 120
risk with reward archetype, 91–92
Roe v. Wade, 16
Romer, Paul, 41
Roots (Haley), 15
Royal Bank of Scotland, 91

Schnur, Jon, 120
secure progress archetype, 88–90
Semco, 196
Semler, Ricardo, 110, 196
Shapiro, Robert, 198
shared desires of X'ers
  definition of success, 71
  desire for career security, 64–66
  desire to be good parents, 67–71
  importance of home, 74
  money views, 66–67
  working mothers and, 68–70
  work/life balance, 71–74
silent generation. *See* Traditionalists
Sinder, R. M., 192
Slacker (movie), 6
small-firm opportunities, 167
SmartPak, 173, 179, 204
star performer syndrome, 127
Stewart, Jon, 5, 36
Stillman, David, 143
Strauss, William, 4, 18, 19, 55, 143, 148, 188, 189
StrengthsFinder, 131
strong ties in networking, 155
Surfing the Edge of Chaos (Milleman and Gioja), 185

Teach For America (TFA), 120
team victory archetype, 90–91

teen years
  the arts and, 13–14
  for Boomers, 49
  diversity issues, 15
  the economy and employment, 8–9
  family and friends, 16–18, 19
  generational characteristics, 3–4
  global awareness and social activism, 14–16
  political events, 9–10
  science and technology, 10–12
  for Traditionalists, 47–48
37signals, 106, 113
Threadless, 176
Title IX, 15
TopCoder, 176
Traditionalists
  demographics, 45
  teen years, 47–48
  view of money, 48–49
  world events, 46–47, 48
Trilogy, 92

urban tribe, 32, 34–35, 155

video games, 12
voices of Gen X
  achieving breadth of experience, 152–154
  back-up jobs, 182–183
  careers and life, 39–40
  dedication to family, 19
  desire for security and self-reliance, 163, 164
  desire to be valued, 133, 140, 166
  distrust of corporations, 9, 65, 66
  entrepreneurship, 165, 170–171, 180–182
  friendships importance, 32–34
  impact of technology and MTV, 12–13
  job-hopping for advancement, 148–149
  job market challenges, 23, 28, 29, 30, 31
  leadership positions, 191–192
  nature of work, 104
  networking, 155–156
  preferred work culture, 202
  relationship with Boomers, 25, 26, 52–53
  relationship with Gen Y, 25–26, 209
  role in the world, 189
  social activism, 14
  switching careers, 121, 122
  taking the initiative, 147
  tolerance for diversity, 16
  work ethic, 24
  working mothers, 68, 70
  work/life balance, 72, 74
  "X sensibility," 13

Watters, Ethan, 32, 155
weak ties in networking, 155
Whole Foods, 91
women in the workforce
  demographics, 73
  during Gen X'ers teen years, 15, 16
  women leaving the workforce, 74
  working mothers, 68–70
women's rights movement, 15
work. *See* career strategies; effectiveness at work; nature of work; organizations; work/life balance
work/life balance
  being smart and lazy, 157–159
  getting engaged with work (*see* engagement at work)
  maintaining flexibility, 160–162
  rethinking your options, 159–160
The World Is Flat (Friedman), 123

Xilinix, 88

Yunus, Muhammad, 107

Zappos, 117

ABOUT THE AUTHOR

Tamara Erickson is both a respected McKinsey Award–winning author and a popular and engaging storyteller. Her compelling views of the future are based on extensive research on changing demographics, employee values, and how successful organizations work. Well-grounded, academically rigorous, and fundamentally optimistic, Tammy's work discerns and describes interesting trends in our future and provides actionable counsel to help both organizations and individuals prepare today.

This book is the third in a trilogy Tammy has written, each exploring how specific generations can excel in today's workplace. *Retire Retirement: Career Strategies for the Boomer Generation* and *Plugged In: The Generation Y Guide to Thriving at Work* were published in 2008.

Tammy (www.TammyErickson.com) coauthored the book *Workforce Crisis: How to Beat the Coming Shortage of Skills and Talent*; five *Harvard Business Review* articles, including "It's Time to Retire Retirement," winner of the McKinsey Award; and an *MIT Sloan Management Review* article. Her blog "Across the Ages" is featured weekly on Harvard Business Digital (http://discussionleader.hbsp.com/erickson/).

She is president of The nGenera Innovation Network (www.ngenera.com) and lives with her family on a farm in Massachusetts.